Introduction to Python for Data Management

Lillian Ren

Preface

Welcome to "Introduction to Python for Data Management." This book aims to introduce the essentials of Python programming and data management in an accessible and engaging manner. It's designed for those new to these topics, offering a straightforward and clear approach.

We start with the basics of Python, guiding you through its installation, syntax and core functionalities. We will explore how to work with data, using practical examples to help you grasp important concepts.

With each chapter, you'll gain practical skills through hands-on examples, building a robust foundation in both programming and data management.

By the end of this book, you will have a solid foundation in both Python programming and data management techniques, ready to tackle more complex challenges.

By fully mastering the contents of this book, you will be well-equipped to pursue entry-level positions in data management or Python programming. This foundation will not only prepare you for initial job roles but also set the stage for further professional growth in these fields.

Let's start this exciting learning journey, paving your way to new career opportunities in the world of Python and data management!

Happy coding and happy data managing!

Lillian Ren

Contents

Chapter 1 Introduction to Python for Data Management

In today's data-driven world, the ability to efficiently manage and analyze data is crucial for making informed decisions and deriving valuable insights. Python, a versatile and powerful programming language, has emerged as a preferred tool for data professionals due to its simplicity, flexibility, and extensive ecosystem of libraries tailored for data manipulation and analysis.

This introduction aims to provide data professionals with a comprehensive overview of Python's capabilities for data management, covering its fundamental concepts, key libraries, and practical applications.

1. Why Python for Data Management?

- Ease of Learning and Use: Python's syntax is intuitive and readable, resembling pseudo-code, which makes it accessible to individuals from various backgrounds, including those without extensive programming experience. Its simplicity accelerates the learning curve, allowing data professionals to quickly grasp concepts and start writing functional code.

- Versatility: Python's versatility extends beyond data management, making it a valuable skill for professionals across different domains. Its broad applicability enables seamless integration with other tools and technologies, fostering interoperability and flexibility in data workflows.

- Rich Ecosystem: Python's ecosystem boasts an extensive collection of libraries and frameworks tailored for diverse data management tasks. From data manipulation and analysis to machine learning and visualization, there's a library available to address virtually every aspect of the data lifecycle.

• Community Support: Python benefits from a vibrant community of developers, data scientists, and enthusiasts who actively contribute to its development and share knowledge through forums, blogs, and open-source projects. This community-driven ethos fosters collaboration and innovation, providing invaluable support to data professionals seeking assistance or guidance.

2. Fundamental Concepts

• Data Structures: Python offers a variety of built-in data structures, each suited for specific data management tasks. Lists, dictionaries, tuples, and sets provide versatile options for organizing and manipulating data, while understanding their characteristics and performance implications is crucial for efficient data processing.

• Functions and Control Flow: Functions encapsulate reusable logic, promoting modularity and code reusability. Control flow structures such as loops and conditionals govern program execution, enabling data professionals to implement iterative processes, conditional logic, and error handling within their scripts.

• File I/O: Python provides robust support for reading from and writing to files in different formats. Libraries like csv, json, pandas, and database connectors facilitate seamless interaction with data stored in various sources, enabling data professionals to import, export, and manipulate data efficiently.

3. Key Libraries for Data Management

- **Pandas:** Pandas is a cornerstone library for data manipulation and analysis in Python. Its DataFrame object provides a powerful and flexible data structure for tabular data, equipped with functions for data selection, filtering, grouping, aggregation, and transformation. Pandas enables data professionals to perform complex data manipulations with ease, facilitating tasks such as data cleaning, transformation, and exploration.

- **NumPy:** NumPy serves as the foundation for numerical computing in Python, offering support for multidimensional arrays and mathematical operations. Its efficient array processing capabilities make it well-suited for numerical computations, statistical analysis, and linear algebra operations commonly encountered in data management tasks.

- Matplotlib and Seaborn: Matplotlib and Seaborn are prominent visualization libraries in Python, enabling data professionals to create a wide range of static and interactive plots, charts, and graphs. These libraries provide extensive customization options, facilitating the creation of insightful visualizations that effectively communicate data insights and trends.

- Scikit-learn: Scikit-learn is a comprehensive machine learning library that provides tools for data preprocessing, model training, evaluation, and deployment. Its user-friendly interface and extensive collection of algorithms make it accessible to data professionals of all skill levels, empowering them to build predictive models and conduct advanced analytics tasks.

4. Practical Applications

- Data Cleaning and Preprocessing: Python facilitates data cleaning and preprocessing tasks by providing libraries like Pandas and NumPy, which offer functions for handling missing values, outliers, duplicates, and inconsistencies. Data professionals can leverage these libraries to prepare data for analysis by standardizing formats, resolving discrepancies, and ensuring data quality.

- Exploratory Data Analysis (EDA): Python enables data exploration through libraries like Pandas, Matplotlib, and Seaborn, which support tasks such as data visualization, descriptive statistics, and pattern identification. EDA allows data professionals to gain insights into data distributions, correlations, and trends, guiding subsequent analysis and hypothesis generation.

- Data Integration and Transformation: Python facilitates data integration and transformation through libraries like Pandas and various file I/O modules, which enable data professionals to extract, transform, and load (ETL) data from disparate sources. Whether working with structured or unstructured data, Python provides tools for merging, reshaping, and cleansing data to prepare it for downstream analysis or consumption.

- Model Development and Evaluation: Python supports the development and evaluation of predictive models through libraries like Scikit-learn, which offer algorithms for classification, regression, clustering, and dimensionality reduction. Data professionals can leverage these libraries to train, validate, and optimize models using best practices in machine learning, enabling data-driven decision-making and predictive analytics.

Before diving into Python for data management, it's essential to grasp some fundamental concepts. Python offers built-in data structures such as lists, dictionaries, tuples, and sets, which are foundational for organizing and manipulating data efficiently. Understanding how to define functions and control flow structures like loops and conditionals enables data professionals to automate repetitive tasks and implement complex data processing logic. Python also provides robust support for reading from and writing to various file formats, including CSV, Excel, JSON, and SQL databases, facilitating seamless interaction with data stored in different sources.

This book will cover the very basic concept of python programming, including syntax, variables, data types, function, object as well as commonly used libraries for data management.

Chapter 2 Install Python and Python Module

1. Download and Install Python

First, please go to Python official website to download the Python exe file.

Download Python:

- Visit the official Python website at https://www.python.org/.
- On the homepage, navigate to the Downloads section.
- You'll see various versions available for download. Choose the latest version appropriate for your operating system. For example, for Windows, you might see options like "Windows Installer" or "Windows x86-64 executable installer" for 64-bit systems.
- Click on the download link for the version you need.

Install Python:

- Once the installer is downloaded, locate the downloaded file and double-click to run it.
- The installation wizard will guide you through the installation process. Click "Next" or "Continue" to proceed through the steps.
- You may be asked to customize the installation by choosing installation options. For most users, the default settings are sufficient. However, make sure to check the option that adds Python to the system PATH. This will allow you to run Python from the command line without specifying its full path.
- Complete the installation by clicking "Install" or "Finish" at the end of the wizard.

Verify Python Installation:
- After installation, open a terminal or command prompt.
- Type python --version or python3 --version and press Enter. This command will display the installed Python version. For example, you might see something like Python 3.9.7. If you see the version number, Python is successfully installed.

Modules and Packages:

Python modules are files containing Python code, while packages are directories containing multiple modules. Modules and packages help organize code into logical units and facilitate code reuse across projects.

```
# Modules and Packages
import math
print(math.sqrt(25))
```

Install Python Modules:
- Open a terminal or command prompt.
- To install a module, use pip, Python's package manager. Type pip install <module_name> and press Enter. Replace <module_name> with the name of the module you want to install.
- For example, to install the popular module numpy, you would type pip install numpy.

  Open your terminal or command prompt and run the following command:

```
pip install module_name
```

Example: to install module pyodbc

```
pip install pyodbc
```

```
C:\Users\lllll1>pip install pyodbc
Requirement already satisfied: pyodbc in c:\users\
```

```
C:\Users\lllll1>pip install pyodbc
Requirement already satisfied: pyodbc in c:\users\lllll1\appdata\local\pac

C:\Users\lllll1>pip3 install -U pyodbc
Requirement already satisfied: pyodbc in c:\users\lllll1\appdata\local\pac
Collecting pyodbc
  Downloading pyodbc-4.0.35-cp310-cp310-win_amd64.whl (66 kB)
                                              66.0/66.0 kB 1.8 MB/s eta 0
Installing collected packages: pyodbc
  Attempting uninstall: pyodbc
    Found existing installation: pyodbc 4.0.34
    Uninstalling pyodbc-4.0.34:
      Successfully uninstalled pyodbc-4.0.34
Successfully installed pyodbc-4.0.35
```

- If you need to install a specific version of a module, you can specify it like pip install <module_name>==<version_number>.
- Pip will download and install the specified module along with any dependencies it requires.

Verify Module Installation:

- After installing a module, you can verify its installation by importing it into a Python script or the Python interpreter.
- Open a Python interpreter by typing python or python3 in the terminal.
- Type import <module_name> and press Enter. If you don't see any error messages, the module is successfully installed.

Upgrade pip (Optional):

- You can upgrade pip to the latest version by running pip install --upgrade pip in the terminal or command prompt. This ensures that you have the latest features and bug fixes in pip itself.

Documente Installed Modules:

- Keep track of the modules you've installed along with their versions. You can maintain this documentation in a text file or any other format that suits your needs. This documentation will be helpful for future reference or sharing with students.

Python is an interpreted scripting language, so it does not need to be compiled. It means it executes the code line by line. Python comes with a *Python Shell (Python Interactive Shell)*. It is used to execute a single python command and get the result.

2. Installing Python IDE

You can use Python Shell like IDLE, PyCharm, Spyder,Visual Studio to write and run your Python codes. In this book, we talk about the Visual Studio Code.

Visual Studio Code

The Python interactive shell is good to try and test small script codes but it will not be for a big project. In a real work environment, developers use different code editors to write codes. Visual studio code is a very popular open source text editor. Please go to the following link to download visual studio https://code.visualstudio.com/

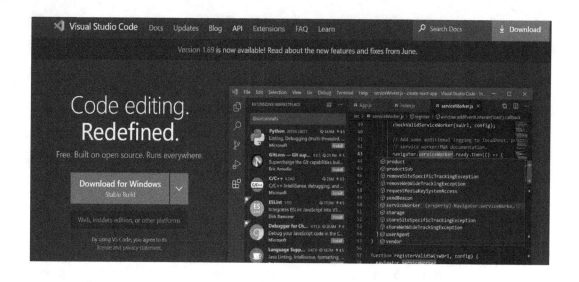

After install Visual Studio Code, you can write codes in Visual Studio:

```
Codes >  Hello.py > ...
  7     print(7 % 2)      # modulus(%)
  8     print(3 // 2)     # Floor division operator(//)
  9
 10     # Checking data types
 11
 12     print(type(10))                              # Int
 13     print(type(3.1415926))                       # Float
 14     print(type(1 +9Kj))                          # Complex
 15     print(type('Apple'))                         # String
 16     print(type([1, 2, 3]))                       # List
 17     print(type({'name':'Nancy'}))               # Dictionary
 18     print(type({9.8, 3.14, 2.7}))               # Set
 19     print(type((9.8, 3.14, 2.7)))               # Tuple
```

3. Using web based platform

If you don't want to install python on your computer, there is an alternative way to run python codes on a web based platform. There are many online platforms. One of this is https://www.online-python.com/

4. How to upgrade Python?

It is very similar way as you first install Python:

Step1: Uninstall old python from your window.

*Tip: This is important. If you have multiple versions of python in your system, you will have a lot of problems later when you start running python codes.

Step 2: Go python official site to download the most recent python installer, the exe file

https://www.python.org/downloads/

Step3: Follow the installer prompts and finish installation

Chapter 3 Basic concepts of python programming

Python programming revolves around several fundamental concepts that form the backbone of the language. These concepts are crucial for understanding how Python works and how to write effective code. Understanding these basic concepts of Python programming is essential for writing clear, concise, and effective code in Python. Mastery of these concepts forms a solid foundation for further exploration and proficiency in Python development.

Here are some basic concepts of Python programming:

1. Syntax

Python syntax is designed to be simple and readable, making it accessible to beginners and experienced programmers alike. Indentation is used to denote code blocks instead of braces or keywords, enhancing readability.Additionally, Python statements end with a newline character, eliminating the need for semicolons. Comments start with the hash symbol (#) and can span multiple lines using triple quotes (''' or """).

```
# Example of indentation
if True:
    print("This statement is indented")
```

2. Variables and Data Types

Variables are used to store data values. Python supports various data types, including integers, floats, strings, booleans, lists, tuples, sets, and dictionaries.

Variables are used to store data values. Python supports various data types:
- Integer: Whole numbers without decimals
- Float: Numbers with decimals
- String: Textual data enclosed within quotes
- Boolean: True or False values
- List: Ordered collection of elements
- Tuple: Ordered, immutable collection of elements
- Set: Unordered collection of unique elements
- Dictionary: Collection of key-value pairs

Example:

```python
# Variables and Data Types
age = 25              # Integer
height = 5.11         # Float
name = "John"         # String
is_student = True     # Boolean
my_list = [1, 2, 3]            # List
my_tuple = (4, 5, 6)           # Tuple
my_set = {1, 2, 3}             # Set
my_dict = {'a': 1, 'b': 2}     # Dictionary
```

3. Operators

Python supports a wide range of operators for performing arithmetic, comparison, logical, and bitwise operations. Examples include +, -, *, / for arithmetic, ==, !=, <, > for comparison, and and, or, not for logical operations.

Python supports various operators for performing operations:
- Arithmetic: +, -, *, /, % (modulus), // (floor division), ** (exponentiation)
- Comparison: ==, !=, <, >, <=, >=
- Logical: and, or, not
- Bitwise: &, |, ^, ~, <<, >>

Example:

```
# Operators
x = 10
y = 5
z = x + y        # Arithmetic
is_equal = x == y  # Comparison
is_valid = x > 0 and y < 10  # Logical
```

4. Control Flow

Control flow statements allow you to control the execution of code based on certain conditions. This includes if-else statements for conditional execution, loops such as for and while loops for iteration, and break and continue statements for altering loop behavior.

```python
# Control Flow
age = 20
if age >= 18:
    print("You are an adult")
else:
    print("You are a minor")


for i in range(5):
    print(i)


num = 0
while num < 5:
    print(num)
    num += 1
```

Control flow allows programmers to dictate the order in which statements are executed in a program. It includes conditional statements (if, elif, else) and loops (for, while) that help in making decisions and repeating tasks based on conditions.

4.1. Conditional Statements:

- if Statement:

- Explain that the if statement allows executing a block of code only if a condition is true.
- Provide examples of simple if statements:

```
x = 10
if x > 5:
    print("x is greater than 5")
```

- if-else Statement:

- Describe how the else statement is used to execute a block of code if the condition in the if statement is false.
- Provide examples of if-else statements:

```
x = 10
if x > 5:
    print("x is greater than 5")
else:
    print("x is less than or equal to 5")
```

- if-elif-else Statement:

- Introduce the elif statement, which allows checking additional conditions if the previous ones are false.
- Provide examples of if-elif-else statements:

```
x = 10
if x > 10:
    print("x is greater than 10")
elif x == 10:
    print("x is equal to 10")
else:
    print("x is less than 10")
```

5. Loops:

- for Loop:

- Explain that the for loop is used to iterate over a sequence (e.g., list, tuple, string) and execute a block of code for each item in the sequence.
- Provide examples of for loops:

```
fruits = ["apple", "banana", "cherry"]
for fruit in fruits:
    print(fruit)
```

- while Loop:

- Describe the while loop, which executes a block of code repeatedly as long as a condition is true.

- Provide examples of while loops:

```python
x = 0
while x < 5:
    print(x)
    x += 1
```

- Loop Control Statements:

- Introduce loop control statements (break, continue, pass) to modify the flow of loops.
- Provide examples of using break , pass and continue within loops.

```python
# Print numbers from 1 to 5 and exit the loop when reaching 3
for i in range(1, 6):
    if i == 3:
        break
    print(i)
```

```python
# Check if a number is even, odd, or zero and do nothing for zero
num = 0

if num == 0:
    pass
elif num % 2 == 0:
    print("Even number")
else:
    print("Odd number")
```

```python
# Print only even numbers from 1 to 5
for i in range(1, 6):
    if i % 2 != 0:  # If number is odd, skip to the next iteration
        continue
    print(i)
```

6. Functions:

Functions are blocks of reusable code that perform a specific task. They help in organizing code, improving readability, and facilitating code reuse. In Python, functions are defined using the def keyword.

```python
# Functions
def greet(name):
    print("Hello, " + name + "!")


greet("Alice")
```

```python
def calculate_rectangle_area(length, width):
    """
    This function calculates the area of a rectangle.
    Parameters:
    length (float): The length of the rectangle.
    width (float): The width of the rectangle.
    Returns:
    float: The area of the rectangle.
    """
    area = length * width
    return area
# Example usage:
length = 5.0
width = 3.0
area = calculate_rectangle_area(length, width)
print("The area of the rectangle is:", area)
```

Ln: 12, Col: 1

▶ Run   ↪ Share   Command Line Arguments

The area of the rectangle is: 15.0

7. Data Structures: Python provides built-in data structures such as lists, tuples, sets, and dictionaries for organizing and storing data efficiently. Understanding how to work with these data structures is essential for effective programming.

Lists:

- Lists are ordered collections of items (elements), which can be of different types.
- Lists are mutable, meaning that you can add, remove, or change items after the list has been created.
- Lists are defined using square brackets [] and elements are separated by commas.
- Example: my_list = [1, 2, 'apple', 'banana']

Tuples:

- Tuples are similar to lists in that they are ordered collections of items. However, unlike lists, tuples are immutable. Once a tuple is created, you cannot modify its contents.
- Tuples are defined using parentheses () and elements are separated by commas.
- Example: my_tuple = (1, 2, 'apple', 'banana')

Sets:

- Sets are unordered collections of unique elements. They are mutable and are useful for storing elements where the order does not matter and duplicates are not allowed.
- Sets are defined using curly braces {} or the set() function.
- Example: my_set = {1, 2, 3, 4}

Dictionaries:

- Dictionaries are collections of key-value pairs, where each key is unique.

- Dictionaries are mutable, which means you can add, remove, or change pairs after the dictionary is created.
- They are defined using curly braces {}, with keys and values separated by a colon :.
- Example: my_dict = {'name': 'John', 'age': 30, 'city': 'New York'} or   my_dict = {'a': 1, 'b': 2}

```python
# Data Structures
my_list = [1, 2, 3]
my_tuple = (4, 5, 6)
my_set = {1, 2, 3}
my_dict = {'a': 1, 'b': 2}
```

7.Input and Output:

Python provides functions for reading input from the user (e.g., input()) and printing output to the console (e.g., print()). Additionally, Python supports file I/O operations for reading from and writing to files.

```python
# Input and Output
name = input("Enter your name: ")
print("Hello, " + name + "!")
```

Exception Handling:

Exception handling allows you to gracefully handle errors and exceptions that may occur during program execution. Python provides try, except, finally, and raise statements for handling exceptions.

```
# Exception Handling
try:
    result = 10 / 0
except ZeroDivisionError:
    print("Error: Division by zero")
```

Object-Oriented Programming (OOP):

Python is an object-oriented programming language, meaning it supports the creation and manipulation of objects. OOP concepts such as classes, objects, inheritance, polymorphism, and encapsulation are integral to Python programming.

```
# Object-Oriented Programming
class Person:
    def __init__(self, name, age):
        self.name = name
        self.age = age

    def greet(self):
        print("Hello, my name is", self.name, "and I am", self.age, "years old.")

person1 = Person("Alice", 25)
person1.greet()
```

Example of class: the result is shown at the bottom under the 'Run' button.

```python
# Object-Oriented Programming
class Person:
    def __init__(self, name, age):
        self.name = name
        self.age = age

    def greet(self):
        print("Hello, my name is", self.name, "and I am", self.age, "years old.")

person1 = Person("Alice", 25)
person1.greet()
```

Ln: 11, Col: 16

▶ Run   ↪ Share   Command Line Arguments

```
Hello, my name is Alice and I am 25 years old.
```

Chapter 4 Introduction to Pandas

1. Pandas Library

As a Python programmer, diving into pandas opens up a rich landscape of data manipulation and analysis capabilities. Pandas is an open-source library that provides high-performance, easy-to-use data structures, and data analysis tools for Python. Its name is derived from the term "panel data," an econometrics term for multidimensional, structured data sets. Here's a concise introduction to what makes pandas a cornerstone in the Python data science ecosystem:

Core Components of Pandas

- DataFrame: This is a two-dimensional, size-mutable, and potentially heterogeneous tabular data structure with labeled axes (rows and columns). Think of it as a spreadsheet or SQL table in Python.
- Series: A one-dimensional labeled array capable of holding any data type (integers, strings, floating point numbers, Python objects, etc.). Each column in a DataFrame is essentially a Series.

Key Features

- Handling Data: Read and write data from various file formats (CSV, Excel, SQL databases, JSON, and more). Pandas can handle a variety of data, including but not limited to: time series, tabular heterogeneous data, arbitrary matrix data with row & column labels.

- Data Cleaning: Provides extensive functions and methods to prepare your data for analysis. It can easily drop missing values, fill missing values with custom logic, and filter data based on conditions.
- Data Transformation: Merge, join, concatenate datasets with ease. Group by functionality to perform split-apply-combine operations on datasets. Pivot and reshape data for comprehensive analysis.
- Analysis: Support for descriptive statistics, aggregation operations, handling time-series data, and custom transformations.
- Performance: Critical code paths are optimized with Cython to improve performance. Operations on large datasets are not only possible but also relatively fast.

2. Getting Started with Pandas

To start using pandas, you need to install it first. If you haven't installed pandas yet, you can do so by running:

```
pip install pandas
```

After installation, you import the pandas library first then you can start using it. Here is a simple example to get a feel for pandas:

```python
import pandas as pd

# Creating a simple DataFrame
data = {'Name': ['John', 'Anna', 'Peter', 'Linda'],
        'Age': [28, 34, 29, 32],
        'City': ['New York', 'Paris', 'Berlin', 'London']}

df = pd.DataFrame(data)

# Display the DataFrame
print(df)

# Basic statistics of numeric columns
print(df.describe())
```

```
      Name  Age       City
0     John   28   New York
1     Anna   34      Paris
2    Peter   29     Berlin
3    Linda   32     London
            Age
count   4.000000
mean   30.750000
std     2.753785
min    28.000000
25%    28.750000
50%    30.500000
75%    32.500000
max    34.000000
```

Pandas is a powerful Python library that provides extensive functionalities for data analysis and manipulation. It's particularly well-suited for dealing with tabular data, where manipulation of columns and rows is common. Below, we explore some key functionalities of pandas with examples, diving into more sophisticated operations you can perform.

2.1 Creating DataFrames

DataFrames are two-dimensional labeled data structures with columns of potentially different types. You can think of it like a spreadsheet or SQL table.

Example: Creating a DataFrame from a Dictionary

```python
import pandas as pd

data = {'Name': ['John', 'Anna', 'Peter', 'Linda'],
        'Age': [28, 34, 29, 32],
        'City': ['New York', 'Paris', 'Berlin', 'London']}
df = pd.DataFrame(data)
print(df)
```

```
    Name  Age      City
0   John   28  New York
1   Anna   34     Paris
2  Peter   29    Berlin
3  Linda   32    London
```

2.2 Reading and Writing Data

Pandas supports various file formats for reading and writing data, including CSV, Excel, JSON, and SQL databases.

Reading from and Writing to CSV

```python
import pandas as pd
# Reading a CSV file
df = pd.read_csv('data.csv')


# Writing to a CSV file, without the index
df.to_csv('output.csv', index=False)
```

Reading from and Writing to xlsx

```
pip install pandas openpyxl
```

```python
import pandas as pd
# Specify the path to your .xlsx file
file_path = 'path_to_your_file.xlsx'


# Read the Excel file
df = pd.read_excel(file_path, engine='openpyxl')
# Display the first few rows of the DataFrame
print(df.head())


# Specify the path where you want to save the .xlsx file
output_file_path = 'path_to_your_output_file.xlsx'
# Write the DataFrame to an Excel file
df.to_excel(output_file_path, index=False, engine='openpyxl')
print(f"DataFrame is written to '{output_file_path}' successfully.")
```

2.3. Reading from and writing to a JSON File

To read data from a JSON file, you can use pd.read_json(). This function converts a JSON string into a pandas DataFrame.

```python
import pandas as pd

# Specify the path to your JSON file
json_file_path = 'data.json'
# Read the JSON file
df = pd.read_json(json_file_path)
# Display the DataFrame
print(df)

# Specify the path where you want to save the JSON file
output_json_file_path = 'output_data.json'

# Write the DataFrame to a JSON file
df.to_json(output_json_file_path, orient='records', lines=True)
print(f"DataFrame is written to '{output_json_file_path}' successfully.")
```

2.4.Reading from CSV/xslx and saving to JSON File

```python
import pandas as pd
# Path to the CSV file
csv_file_path = 'your_data.csv'
# Read the CSV file
df = pd.read_csv(csv_file_path)


# Read the xslx file
#df = pd.read_excel(file_path, engine='openpyxl')
# Display the first few rows to verify the data
print(df.head())


# Path where the JSON file will be saved
json_file_path = 'output_data.json'
# Convert the DataFrame to JSON and save it to a file
df.to_json(json_file_path, orient='records', lines=True)
print(f"Data has been written to '{json_file_path}' successfully.")
```

3. Data Selection and Manipulation

3.1 Data Selection and Filtering

Selecting specific data from a DataFrame is a common operation, which can be done based on labels, integer location, or conditions.

Example: Selecting Rows Based on Conditions

```python
# Selecting rows where Age is greater than 30
older_than_30 = df[df['Age'] > 30]
print(older_than_30)
```

3.4. Handling Missing Data

Pandas provides convenient methods to detect, remove, or fill missing data with na.

Example1: Filling Missing Values with mean of age

```python
# Assuming 'df' contains missing values
df_filled = df.fillna(value={'Age': df['Age'].mean()})
print(df_filled)
```

Example2: Filling missing values with zero

```python
# Filling missing values
df_filled = df.fillna(value=0)
```

Example3: Dropping rows with any missing values

```python
# Dropping rows with any missing values
df_dropped = df.dropna()
```

3.5. Data Aggregation and Group Operations

Grouping data based on certain criteria and then applying aggregation functions is a powerful data analysis mechanism.

Example: Grouping and Aggregating

```python
# Group by 'City' and calculate mean 'Age'
mean_age_by_city = df.groupby('City')['Age'].mean()
print(mean_age_by_city)
```

3.6. Merging and Concatenating Data

Pandas provides functionalities to combine datasets in various ways, such as merging (similar to SQL joins) and concatenating along an axis.

Example: Merging DataFrames

```python
import pandas as pd
df1 = pd.DataFrame({'EmployeeID': [1, 2, 3], 'Name': ['John', 'Anna', 'Peter']})
df2 = pd.DataFrame({'EmployeeID': [1, 2, 4], 'Salary': [50000, 60000, 40000]})

# Merging on 'EmployeeID'
merged_df = pd.merge(df1, df2, on='EmployeeID', how='inner')
print(merged_df)
```

```
   EmployeeID  Name  Salary
0           1  John   50000
1           2  Anna   60000
```

3. 7. Pivot Tables

Pivot tables are useful for summarizing and analyzing data in DataFrame format, similar to Excel pivot tables.

Example: Creating a Pivot Table

```python
import pandas as pd
data = {'Date': ['2020-01-01', '2020-01-02', '2020-01-02', '2020-01-03'],
        'City': ['New York', 'Los Angeles', 'New York', 'Los Angeles'],
        'Temperature': [32, 75, 30, 77]}
df = pd.DataFrame(data)


pivot = pd.pivot_table(df, values='Temperature', index='Date', columns='City', aggfunc='mean')
print(pivot)
```

```
City          Los Angeles  New York
Date
2020-01-01            NaN      32.0
2020-01-02           75.0      30.0
2020-01-03           77.0       NaN
```

3.8. Data reshaping

Melting wide format to long format

Melting is used to transform data from wide format to long format, making it easier to analyze or plot. Converting data from wide format to long format can be efficiently done using the `pandas` library in Python, specifically with the `melt` function. The "melting" process transforms a dataset from having multiple columns representing different variables (wide format) to a format where there is one column that contains all the variable names and another column that contains the values (long format).

```python
import pandas as pd

# Sample DataFrame in wide format
data = {
    'ID': [1, 2, 3],
    'MeasurementA_2020': [20, 21, 19],
    'MeasurementA_2021': [22, 20, 21],
    'MeasurementB_2020': [30, 31, 29],
    'MeasurementB_2021': [32, 30, 31],
}
df_wide = pd.DataFrame(data)

# Melting the DataFrame
df_long = pd.melt(df_wide, id_vars=['ID'],
var_name='Measurement_Year', value_name='Value')

print(df_long)
```

The wide format	The result of long format

`'ID': [1, 2, 3],`
`'MeasurementA_2020': [20, 21, 19],`
`'MeasurementA_2021': [22, 20, 21],`
`'MeasurementB_2020': [30, 31, 29],`
`'MeasurementB_2021': [32, 30, 31],`
	<pre> ID Measurement_Year Value
	0 1 MeasurementA_2020 20
	1 2 MeasurementA_2020 21
	2 3 MeasurementA_2020 19
	3 1 MeasurementA_2021 22
	4 2 MeasurementA_2021 20
	5 3 MeasurementA_2021 21
	6 1 MeasurementB_2020 30
	7 2 MeasurementB_2020 31
	8 3 MeasurementB_2020 29
	9 1 MeasurementB_2021 32
	10 2 MeasurementB_2021 30
	11 3 MeasurementB_2021 31</pre>

Stacking

Stacking in pandas is a method to reshape data by pivoting the innermost column index levels to become the innermost row index levels. Stacking pivots a level of column labels to the row index, returning a DataFrame with a new innermost level of row index.

```
import pandas as pd

# Creating a DataFrame with multi-level columns
index = ['Store 1', 'Store 2', 'Store 3']
columns = pd.MultiIndex.from_tuples([
    ('Product A', '2020'),
    ('Product A', '2021'),
    ('Product B', '2020'),
    ('Product B', '2021'),
], names=['Product', 'Year'])

data = [
    [100, 110, 90, 95],  # Sales data for Store 1
    [150, 160, 140, 145],  # Sales data for Store 2
    [200, 210, 190, 195],  # Sales data for Store 3
]

df = pd.DataFrame(data, index=index, columns=columns)
print("Multilevel data frame:\n",df)
# Stacking the 'Year' level
df_stacked = df.stack(level='Year')

print("Stacking at the 'Year' level\n",df_stacked)
```

| ```
Multilevel data frame:
  Product Product A       Product B
Year           2020 2021      2020 2021
Store 1         100  110        90   95
Store 2         150  160       140  145
Store 3         200  210       190  195
``` | ```
Stacking at the 'Year' level
  Product          Product A  Product B
       Year
Store 1 2020           100         90
        2021           110         95
Store 2 2020           150        140
        2021           160        145
Store 3 2020           200        190
        2021           210        195
``` |

Unstacking

Unstacking in pandas is the inverse operation of stacking, which moves a level of the index to the columns, thereby "widening" the DataFrame. This operation is particularly useful when you need to pivot a portion of the data structured in a long format back into a wide format for analysis or reporting purposes.

```
# Unstacking the DataFrame
# This operation will move one of the levels of the row index back to the
columns

# For the purpose of demonstration, let's simulate the stacked DataFrame
quickly
import pandas as pd
import numpy as np

# Example multi-level index from stacked data (Month, Product, Year)
index = pd.MultiIndex.from_product([
    ['January', 'February'],  # Simplified for demonstration
    ['Product A', 'Product B'],
    ['2019', '2020']
], names=['Month', 'Product', 'Year'])
```

```
# Example data
data = np.random.randint(80, 200, size=(len(index), 1))  # Sales data

# Create the DataFrame
df_stacked = pd.DataFrame(data, index=index, columns=['Sales'])

# Now, let's unstack the 'Year' level to move it back to the columns
df_unstacked = df_stacked.unstack(level='Year')

print(df_unstacked)
```

stacked data frame	Unstacked data frame

<pre>   Sales
Month   Product   Year
January   Product A 2019   145
                    2020   104
          Product B 2019   188
                    2020   136
February Product A 2019   144
                    2020   157
          Product B 2019   87
                    2020   152</pre>
	<pre> Sales
	Year 2019 2020
	Month Product
	February Product A 144 157
	          Product B 87 152
	January Product A 145 104
	          Product B 188 136</pre>

4. Looping through multiple files and combine data

Looping through multiple files to combine their data into a single DataFrame
is a common task in data analysis, especially when dealing with data split
across several files with a similar structure. Here's how you can do this using
pandas in Python:

Scenario

Assume you have multiple CSV files named data1.csv, data2.csv, data3.csv, etc., located in the same directory. Each file has the same structure (i.e., the same columns), and you want to combine them into a single DataFrame.

Step-by-Step Solution

1.List Files in Directory: Use the glob module to list all CSV files in the directory.

2. Read and Append Data: Loop through the list of files, read each file into a DataFrame, and append it to a list of DataFrames.

3. Concatenate DataFrames: Use **pd.concat()** to concatenate all DataFrames in the list into a single DataFrame.

Example Code

```python
import pandas as pd
import glob


path = 'path/to/your/csv/files'
all_files = glob.glob(path + "/*.csv")


#Define an empty List as space holder  to hold data from each file


dfs = [  ]



for filename in all_files:


    df = pd.read_csv(filename)
```

```
    dfs.append(df)



combined_df = pd.concat(dfs, ignore_index=True)



print(combined_df)
```

Notes:

- The ignore_index=True parameter in pd.concat() is used to reindex the new combined DataFrame. If your files contain a meaningful index that you wish to preserve, you might want to omit this parameter.
- If your CSV files have different structures (different columns) and you want to combine them, you'll need to ensure alignment of the columns either by specifying which columns to use from each file or by standardizing the structure before concatenating.
- This example uses CSV files, but pandas supports various other file formats (e.g., Excel, JSON, SQL databases). The approach would be similar, with the reading function changed according to the file format (e.g., pd.read_excel for Excel files).

This method is efficient for combining data from multiple files, allowing for easy manipulation and analysis of the combined dataset with pandas.

You can also use OS library to complete the same task:

```python
directory = 'path/to/your/csv/files'
all_files = os.listdir(directory)


dataframes_list = []

for file in all_files:

    file_path = os.path.join(directory, file)

    if file_path.endswith('.csv'):

        df = pd.read_csv(file_path)
        dataframes_list.append(df)


combined_df = pd.concat(dataframes_list, ignore_index=True)


print(combined_df)
```

Another example is to create Python codes that search for files within a directory (and optionally, its subdirectories) that contain a specific string in their filenames and then renames those files.

```python
import os

def search_and_rename_files(directory, match_string, new_string,
include_subdirs=False):
    # Check if subdirectories should be included in the search
    if include_subdirs:
        pattern = '**/*'
    else:
        pattern = '*'

    # Walk through the directory
    for root, dirs, files in os.walk(directory):
        for filename in files:
            # Check if the file contains the matching string
            if match_string in filename:
                # Construct the new filename
                new_filename = filename.replace(match_string, new_string)
                # Construct full file paths
                old_file_path = os.path.join(root, filename)
                new_file_path = os.path.join(root, new_filename)
                # Rename the file
                os.rename(old_file_path, new_file_path)
                print(f"Renamed '{old_file_path}' to '{new_file_path}'")

        if not include_subdirs:
```

```
        # If we're not including subdirectories, break after the first iteration
        break

# Example usage
directory_path = '/path/to/directory'
match_string = 'old_text'
new_string = 'new_text'
search_and_rename_files(directory_path, match_string, new_string,
include_subdirs=True)
```

5. Getting it right in file path

We used to the back slash in file path in both windows and IOS platform
C:\Users\OneDrive\Documents\.

In Python, the backslash (\) is a special character used to represent certain
whitespace characters, like \n for newline or \t for tab. So, when you're using
backslashes in file paths on Windows, Python interprets these as escape
characters. This can lead to errors or unexpected behavior if your path
contains sequences that accidentally form valid escape sequences, like \n or
\t.

To correctly use backslashes in file paths in Python, you have several options:

1. Double Backslashes

Use two backslashes to represent a single backslash in the path. The first backslash escapes the second one, telling Python to treat it as a literal backslash rather than as the start of an escape sequence.

"C:\\Users\\YourName\\Documents\\file.txt"

2. Raw Strings

Prefix the string with r to create a raw string, which tells Python to ignore escape sequences within the string. This is often the easiest way to deal with Windows paths.

r"C:\Users\YourName\Documents\file.txt"

3. Forward Slashes

Python and many of its libraries (like os and pathlib) normalize file paths, so you can often use forward slashes (/) instead of backslashes. This avoids the issue entirely.

"C:/Users/YourName/Documents/file.txt"

Personally, I prefer using forward slashes in Python consistently to avoid any problems.

Chapter 5 Introduction to Numpy

NumPy is a fundamental package for scientific computing in Python. It stands for Numerical Python, is a library that provides support for arrays, matrices, and high-level mathematical functions to operate on these data structures. NumPy is widely used in the fields of science, engineering, and data analysis because it offers an efficient interface for storing and manipulating large datasets in a way that is both convenient and accessible.

1. **Core Features of NumPy**

    Multidimensional Arrays: At the heart of NumPy is the array object, a fast and flexible container for large datasets in Python. Arrays in NumPy can have any number of dimensions, allowing for efficient operation on vectors, matrices, and higher-dimensional datasets.

    Array Operations: NumPy provides a comprehensive set of mathematical functions to perform operations on arrays. This includes basic arithmetic, linear algebra, statistical operations, and much more. These operations are performed element-wise and are optimized for speed and memory efficiency.

    Broadcasting: Broadcasting is a powerful mechanism that allows NumPy to work with arrays of different shapes during arithmetic operations. It enables automatic shaping of data to match, making coding faster and more intuitive without sacrificing performance.

Integration with Other Libraries: NumPy arrays serve as the foundational data structure for many other libraries in the Python ecosystem, including SciPy (for advanced math, science, and engineering), Matplotlib (for plotting and visualization), and Pandas (for data analysis and manipulation). This integration facilitates a seamless workflow for data analysis and scientific computing.

2. Getting Started with NumPy

To get started with NumPy, you first need to install it. It can be installed via pip, the Python package manager, with the following command:

```
pip install numpy
```

When using numpy, import in the beginning of the python file.

```
import numpy as np
```

3. Array Creation

NumPy offers several functions to create arrays.

3.1. Create arrays filled with constant values from Python Lists or Tuples

```python
import numpy as np
a = np.array([1, 2, 3])  # Create an array from a list
print("Array a:\n",a)
b = np.zeros((2, 3))  # Create an array of zeros with shape (2,3)
c = np.ones((3, 4), dtype=np.float64)  # Create an array of ones with specified dtype
d = np.full((2, 2), 7)  # Create a constant array filled with 7
print("Array b:\n", b)
print("Array c:\n", c)
print("Array d:\n", d)
```

Ln: 9, Col: 23

▶ Run   ↪ Share   Command Line Arguments

```
Array a:
 [1 2 3]
Array b:
 [[0. 0. 0.]
 [0. 0. 0.]]
Array c:
 [[1. 1. 1. 1.]
 [1. 1. 1. 1.]
 [1. 1. 1. 1.]]
Array d:
 [[7 7]
 [7 7]]
```

3.2. Create arrays filled with sequences of numbers

```python
import numpy as np
A = np.arange(10)  # Similar to Python's range but returns an array
B = np.linspace(0, 1, num=5)  # Create an array of five values evenly spaced between 0 and 1
print("Array A:\n", A)
print("Array B:\n", B)
```

Ln: 6, Col: 1

▶ Run   ↱ Share   Command Line Arguments

```
Array A:
 [0 1 2 3 4 5 6 7 8 9]
Array B:
 [0.   0.25 0.5  0.75 1.  ]


** Process exited - Return Code: 0 **
Press Enter to exit terminal
```

3.3. Create Identity matrix

```
main.py    +

1    import numpy as np
2    AA = np.eye(4)  # Create a 4x4 identity matrix
3    print("Array AA:\n", AA)
4
5
```

Ln: 4, Col: 1

▶ Run   ↪ Share   Command Line Arguments

```
Array AA:
 [[1. 0. 0. 0.]
 [0. 1. 0. 0.]
 [0. 0. 1. 0.]
 [0. 0. 0. 1.]]
```

4. Array Operations

NumPy supports a wide range of operations on arrays:

4.1. Element-wise operations

Operations are performed element-wise without explicitly writing loops. This is not only more concise but also faster.

```
main.py    +

1   import numpy as np
2   a = np.array([1, 2, 3])
3   b = np.array([4, 5, 6])
4   print("a + b:\n",a + b)   # Element-wise addition
5   print("a * b:\n",a * b)   # Element-wise multiplication
6
7   c = np.array([1, 2, 3])
8   print("c:\n",c + 10)   # Adds 10 to each element
9

Ln: 8,  Col: 14

  ▶ Run      ↱ Share    Command Line Arguments

  a + b:
   [5 7 9]
  a * b:
   [ 4 10 18]
  c:
   [11 12 13]
```

4.2. Aggregations

NumPy provides functions to perform statistical calculations on arrays, like
sum, mean, max, min, and many more.

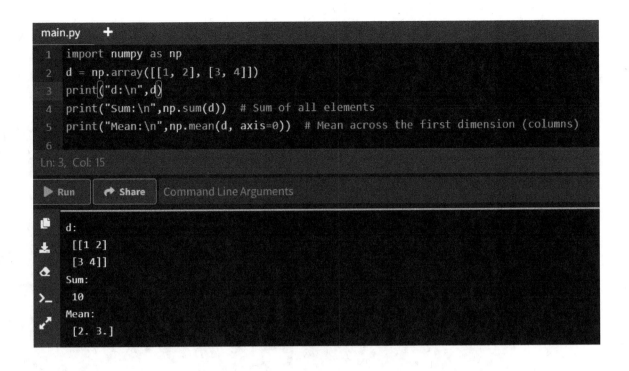

```
main.py                +
1  import numpy as np
2  d = np.array([[1, 2], [3, 4]])
3  print("d:\n",d)
4  print("Sum:\n",np.sum(d))   # Sum of all elements
5  print("Mean:\n",np.mean(d, axis=0))   # Mean across the first dimension (columns)
6
Ln: 3, Col: 15
```

▶ Run   ↷ Share   Command Line Arguments

```
d:
 [[1 2]
 [3 4]]
Sum:
 10
Mean:
 [2. 3.]
```

4.3. Indexing and Slicing

NumPy arrays support complex indexing and slicing operations:

Basic slicing: Similar to Python lists but can be multidimensional.

```
main.py    +
1    import numpy as np
2    e = np.array([[1, 2, 3], [4, 5, 6]])
3    print('e:\n',e)
4    print(e[0, 1])   # Access element at row 0, column 1
5    print(e[:, 1])   # Access the second column
6
```
Ln: 3, Col: 15

▶ Run   ↪ Share   Command Line Arguments

```
e:
 [[1 2 3]
 [4 5 6]]
2
[2 5]
```

5. Linear Algebra Operations

NumPy provides a set of functions for linear algebra operations:

Matrix multiplication: Using the dot function or @ operator.

```
main.py  +
1  import numpy as np
2  f = np.array([[1, 2,3], [4, 5,6]])
3  g = np.array([[10, 11], [20, 21],[30,31]])
4  print('f:\n',f)
5  print('g:\n',g)
6  print('f*g:\n',f.dot(g))  # Matrix multiplication
Ln: 6,  Col: 50
```

▶ Run   ↪ Share   Command Line Arguments

```
f:
 [[1 2 3]
 [4 5 6]]
g:
 [[10 11]
 [20 21]
 [30 31]]
f*g:
 [[140 146]
 [320 335]]
```

To check the result,let's refresh the matrix multiplication rules:

$$\begin{bmatrix} 1 & 2 & 3 \\ 4 & 5 & 6 \end{bmatrix} \times \begin{bmatrix} 10 & 11 \\ 20 & 21 \\ 30 & 31 \end{bmatrix}$$

$$= \begin{bmatrix} 1\times10 + 2\times20 + 3\times30 & 1\times11 + 2\times21 + 3\times31 \\ 4\times10 + 5\times20 + 6\times30 & 4\times11 + 5\times21 + 6\times31 \end{bmatrix}$$

$$= \begin{bmatrix} 10+40+90 & 11+42+93 \\ 40+100+180 & 44+105+186 \end{bmatrix} = \begin{bmatrix} 140 & 146 \\ 320 & 335 \end{bmatrix}$$

6. Random Number Generation

NumPy also includes a robust random number generation package:

Get simple random data: np.random.rand, np.random.randint, etc.

Here is an example to get a random number from a range between a and b(100 and 120). You can change the value of a and b as you preferred.

```python
import numpy as np
a = 100
b = 120
c = np.random.randint(a, b)
print("The random number between a and b is:",c)
```

Ln: 8, Col: 1

▶ Run   ↪ Share   Command Line Arguments

The random number between a and b is: 105

Shuffling Arrays

To shuffle an array (i.e., to randomly rearrange the elements in an array), you can use random.shuffle(). This function shuffles the array in place, meaning the original array is modified.

```python
import numpy as np
my_array = [1, 2, 3, 4, 5]
print("The original array is:",my_array)

np.random.shuffle(my_array)
print("The shuffled array is:",my_array)
```

Ln: 9, Col: 1

▶ Run   ↱ Share   Command Line Arguments

```
The original array is: [1, 2, 3, 4, 5]
The shuffled array is: [5, 3, 4, 1, 2]
```

Each time you run the code, the order of the shuffled array is different.

Here is the result after another run.

```
The original array is: [1, 2, 3, 4, 5]
The shuffled array is: [3, 4, 2, 5, 1]
```

You can also use a random library only without Numpy library to perform the same to shuffle the array.

```python
import random
my_array = [1, 2, 3, 4, 5]
print("The original array is:",my_array)


random.shuffle(my_array)
print("The shuffled array is:",my_array)

```

Ln: 6, Col: 1

▶ Run   ↪ Share   Command Line Arguments

```
The original array is: [1, 2, 3, 4, 5]
The shuffled array is: [5, 1, 3, 2, 4]
```

Generate permutations

Generating all possible permutations of a sequence in Python can be done using the `itertools.permutations()` function from the `itertools` module. This function produces an iterator over all possible permutations of a given sequence.

```python
import itertools

# Define the sequence
sequence = [1, 2, 3]

# Generate all permutations of the sequence
perms = itertools.permutations(sequence)

# Print each permutation
for perm in perms:
    print(perm)

```

Ln: 13, Col: 5

▶ Run   ↪ Share   Command Line Arguments

```
(1, 2, 3)
(1, 3, 2)
(2, 1, 3)
(2, 3, 1)
(3, 1, 2)
(3, 2, 1)
```

Generating All Permutations with NumPy

For generating all permutations, you essentially have to rely on `itertools.permutations` and then convert each permutation to a NumPy array if you need NumPy array functionalities:

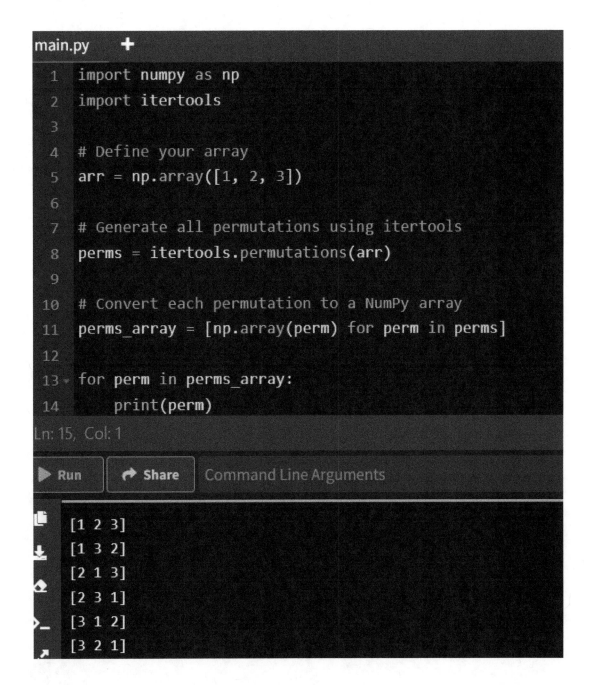

```
main.py        +
1   import numpy as np
2   import itertools
3
4   # Define your array
5   arr = np.array([1, 2, 3])
6
7   # Generate all permutations using itertools
8   perms = itertools.permutations(arr)
9
10  # Convert each permutation to a NumPy array
11  perms_array = [np.array(perm) for perm in perms]
12
13  for perm in perms_array:
14      print(perm)
```
Ln: 15, Col: 1

▶ Run   ↱ Share   Command Line Arguments

```
[1 2 3]
[1 3 2]
[2 1 3]
[2 3 1]
[3 1 2]
[3 2 1]
```

Distributions:

Generate data following a variety of statistical distributions like normal (np.random.normal), uniform (np.random.uniform), etc.

You can use the python codes to generate random numbers following normal distribution, and get the distribution plot.

```python
import numpy as np
# Parameters for the distribution
mean = 0  # Mean of the distribution
std_dev = 1  # Standard deviation of the distribution
num_samples = 1000  # Number of samples to generate

# Generate random data
data = np.random.normal(loc=mean, scale=std_dev, size=num_samples)

import matplotlib.pyplot as plt

# Create a histogram of the data
plt.hist(data, bins=30, density=True, alpha=0.6, color='g')

# Plot the distribution curve
xmin, xmax = plt.xlim()
x = np.linspace(xmin, xmax, 100)
p = np.exp(-((x - mean) ** 2) / (2 * std_dev ** 2)) / (std_dev * np.sqrt(2 *
np.pi))
plt.plot(x, p, 'k', linewidth=2)

title = "Fit results: mean = %.2f,  std = %.2f" % (mean, std_dev)
plt.title(title)

plt.show()
```

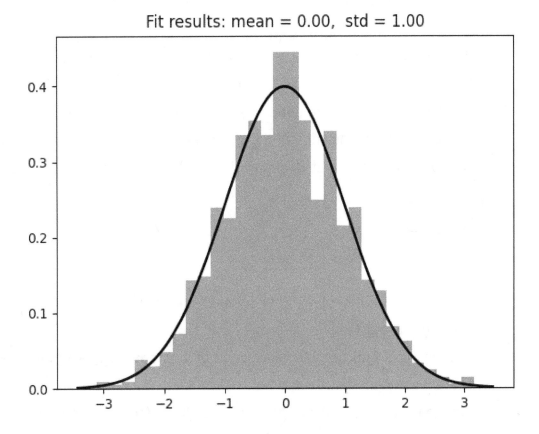

Fit results: mean = 0.00, std = 1.00

7.Difference between Pandas and Numpy

Pandas and NumPy are two of the most fundamental libraries in the Python data science and analytics ecosystem, each with its specialized focus and capabilities. While they share some functionalities, there are significant differences between them. Understanding these differences is crucial for selecting the most appropriate tool for a given task.

NumPy provides an efficient N-dimensional array object (ndarray) that allows for efficient manipulation of large arrays of homogenous data.

Pandas, on the other hand, is built on top of NumPy and offers data structures and data analysis tools that make it easy to manipulate, aggregate, and visualize data. The two primary data structures in Pandas are Series (1-dimensional) and DataFrame (2-dimensional), which can hold heterogenous data; that is, each column can have its own data type.

NumPy Key Features:

- Efficient Array Computing: Fast, memory-efficient multidimensional array object (ndarray).
- Mathematical Functions: A wide range of mathematical functions to perform operations on arrays.
- Broadcasting Capabilities: Rules for applying operations on arrays of different sizes and shapes.
- Linear Algebra, Random Number Generation, and Fourier Transform: Built-in functions for advanced mathematical operations.

NumPy Use Cases:

- Mathematical operations on large datasets.
- Matrix multiplications and linear algebra.
- Signal processing and statistical analysis.

Pandas Key Features:

- DataFrames and Series: Flexible data structures for handling tabular data.
- Data Alignment and Missing Data Handling: Automatic alignment of data and sophisticated handling of missing values.
- Powerful Data Manipulation Tools: Easy-to-use functions for filtering, grouping, and pivoting data.
- Time Series Functionality: Extensive support for date and time-based indexing, resampling, and time series analysis.
- Read and Write Support: Tools for reading and writing data in different formats like CSV, Excel, SQL, and more.

Pandas Use Cases:

- Data cleaning and transformation.
- Exploratory data analysis and visualization.
- Statistical modeling and data analysis.
- Handling time-series data.

Key Differences

- Data Structures: NumPy's main data structure is the ndarray for numerical computing, whereas Pandas provides Series and DataFrame for handling heterogenous data.
- Performance: For operations involving large arrays of numerical data, NumPy is generally more efficient due to its underlying implementation. However, Pandas is more optimized for tabular data operations, such as joins, concatenations, and groupings.
- Data Types: NumPy arrays have one dtype for the entire array, while Pandas DataFrames allow for each column to have a separate dtype.

- Indexing: Pandas provides more powerful indexing options, including label-based indexing, multi-indexing, and more sophisticated data manipulation techniques.
- Purpose: NumPy is more suited for numerical and mathematical computations. Pandas, with its rich functionality for data manipulation and analysis, is better suited for data munging, preparation, and analysis tasks.

In practice, Pandas and NumPy are often used together in data analysis workflows: NumPy for efficient computation on numerical data, and Pandas for high-level data manipulation and analysis.

8. Example of renaming files in a folder with adding a prefix:

```
import os

# Path to the directory containing the files
folder_path = '/path/to/your/folder'

# Prefix to add
prefix = 'new_'

# List all files in the folder
for filename in os.listdir(folder_path):
    if filename.endswith('.txt'):  # Check for .txt files
        # Construct the new filename
        new_filename = prefix + filename
        # Construct the full file paths
        old_file = os.path.join(folder_path, filename)
        new_file = os.path.join(folder_path, new_filename)
        # Rename the file
        os.rename(old_file, new_file)
        print(f'Renamed "{filename}" to "{new_filename}"')
```

Chapter 6 Web scraping, downloading and Connecting databases

1. Web scraping

Web scraping is the process of programmatically retrieving information from websites. This technique is used to extract large amounts of data from websites, which is then saved to a local file or database. It's used for various purposes, such as price comparison, job monitoring, research, and much more. Python, with its rich ecosystem, offers several libraries to facilitate web scraping, such as requests for making HTTP requests, BeautifulSoup and lxml for parsing HTML and XML documents, and Scrapy, a powerful framework for extracting the data, monitoring, and automating web crawls.

1.1 Steps in Web Scraping

Identify the Target Website(s): Determine which website(s) contain the data you want to scrape. It's crucial to review the website's terms of service and robots.txt file to understand the guidelines and restrictions on web scraping activities.

Inspecting the Page: Use tools like the developer tools in Firefox or Chrome to inspect the structure of the website and identify how the data is structured.

Requesting the Page: Utilize a Python library such as requests to retrieve the page content.

Parsing the Content: Use a library like BeautifulSoup to parse the HTML/XML content of the page and extract the relevant information.

Storing the Data: Save the scraped data into a structured form such as CSV, JSON, or a database.

Respectful Scraping: It's important to be respectful and not overload the website's server by making too many requests too quickly. Use time delays and respect the robots.txt file guidelines.

Example: Scraping Quotes from a Website

Let's say we want to scrape quotes from a hypothetical website that lists famous quotes. We would use requests to fetch the page and BeautifulSoup to parse and extract the quotes.

Note: The following is a hypothetical example for educational purposes. Always check a website's scraping policy before proceeding.

```python
import requests
from bs4 import BeautifulSoup

# Target URL
url = 'http://quotes.toscrape.com/'

# Make a request to the website
response = requests.get(url)
html = response.content

# Parse the HTML content
soup = BeautifulSoup(html, 'html.parser')

# Extract quotes from the parsed HTML
quotes = soup.find_all('span', class_='text')

# Print each quote
for quote in quotes:
    print(quote.text)
```

2. Downloading Files from the Web

Downloading files, such as PDFs, text, csv files, excel file or images, can be done using the **requests** library. Here's a simple example to download an image:

```python
import requests

# URL of the file to be downloaded
file_url = "http://example.com/image.png"

# Send a HTTP request to the server and save the HTTP response in a
response object
response = requests.get(file_url)

# Open a local file with write-binary ('wb') permission and write the
contents of the response
with open("downloaded_image.png", 'wb') as file:
    file.write(response.content)
```

This basic framework for web scraping and downloading files can be adapted for more complex scenarios, including handling login authentication, navigating through pages, and dealing with JavaScript-rendered content using libraries like **Selenium** or **Pyppeteer.**

Basic Selenium Script for Web Scraping:

Here's an example of how to use Selenium to scrape quotes from "http://quotes.toscrape.com/", similar to the earlier BeautifulSoup example:

```python
from selenium import webdriver
from selenium.webdriver.common.by import By
from selenium.webdriver.chrome.service import Service
import time

# Path to where you've saved your WebDriver executable
webdriver_path = '/path/to/your/webdriver/chromedriver'

# Set up WebDriver
service = Service(webdriver_path)
driver = webdriver.Chrome(service=service)

# Navigate to the webpage
driver.get('http://quotes.toscrape.com/')

# Allow time for the page to load
time.sleep(5)

# Locate the quotes and print them out
quotes = driver.find_elements(By.CLASS_NAME, 'text')
for quote in quotes:
    print(quote.text)

# Clean up by closing the browser window
driver.quit()
```

Selenium is a powerful tool for web scraping, especially on websites that are heavily dependent on JavaScript. However, it's generally slower than using requests and BeautifulSoup due to the overhead of running a web browser. Use it when you need to interact with web pages or scrape dynamically generated content.

3.Connecting to Microsoft SQL Server database

Connecting to a Microsoft SQL Server database from Python can be done using several libraries, but one of the most popular and straightforward methods is through the **pyodbc** library. Here's a general approach to establish a connection and interact with an MS SQL database:

Step 1: Install pyodbc

First, ensure that **pyodbc** is installed in your Python environment. You can install it using pip:

```
pip install pyodbc
```

Step 2: Import pyodbc

In your Python script or interactive session, import the pyodbc library:

```
import pyodbc
```

Step 3: Connection String

To connect to the database, you'll need a connection string. The connection string contains information about the database driver, server, database name, user ID, and password.

```
conn_str = (
    "Driver={SQL Server};"
    "Server=your_server_address;"
    "Database=your_database_name;"
    "UID=your_username;"
    "PWD=your_password;"
)
```

If your SQL Server instance uses Windows Authentication, you might add connection string like:"Trusted_Connection=yes;"

Step 4: Establish Connection

Use the connection string to establish a connection to the database:

```
conn = pyodbc.connect(conn_str)
```

Step 5: Create a Cursor Object

Once connected, you can create a cursor object using the connection. This cursor is used to execute SQL queries.

```
cursor = conn.cursor()
```

Step 6: Execute SQL Queries

You can now execute SQL queries using the cursor object. For example, to create and update table:

```
# Create a new table
cursor.execute('''
CREATE TABLE Employees (
    EmployeeID int PRIMARY KEY,
    FirstName varchar(255),
    LastName varchar(255),
    Department varchar(255)
)
''')
conn.commit()  # Commit the transaction


# Update a table (adding a new column here)
cursor.execute('''
ALTER TABLE Employees
ADD BirthDate date
''')
conn.commit()
```

to select data and insert data

```
import pyodbc

# Set up the database connection
conn = pyodbc.connect(
    r'Driver={SQL Server};'
    r'Server=your_server_name;'
    r'Database=your_database_name;'
    r'UID=your_username;'
    r'PWD=your_password;'
)
cursor = conn.cursor()

# Execute a SELECT query
cursor.execute('SELECT EmployeeID, FirstName, LastName FROM
```

Employees')

```
# Fetch all rows from the query
rows = cursor.fetchall()

# Iterate over the rows to print the data
for row in rows:
    print(f"Employee ID: {row.EmployeeID}, First Name: {row.FirstName},
Last Name: {row.LastName}")

# Close the connection
conn.close()
```

To insert or update data, you might use:

```
# Insert data into the table
cursor.execute('''
INSERT INTO Employees (EmployeeID, FirstName, LastName, Department)
VALUES (?, ?, ?, ?)''', (1, 'John', 'Doe', 'HR'))
conn.commit()

# Query data
cursor.execute('SELECT * FROM Employees')
rows = cursor.fetchall()
for row in rows:
    print(row)
```

For more complex data retrieval, you might use JOIN to combine data from multiple tables, or GROUP BY to aggregate data:

```
# Query with JOIN
cursor.execute('''
SELECT Employees.FirstName, Employees.LastName,
Departments.DeptName
```

```
FROM Employees
JOIN Departments ON Employees.DepartmentID =
Departments.DepartmentID
"")

# Query with GROUP BY and aggregate functions
cursor.execute('''
SELECT Department, COUNT(*) AS NumEmployees
FROM Employees
GROUP BY Department
"")

# Close the connection
conn.close()
```

Step 7: Close the Connection

It's important to close the connection to the database when you're done to free
up resources:

```
cursor.execute("INSERT INTO your_table_name (column1, column2) VALUES (?, ?)", (value1, value2))
conn.commit()  # Commit the transaction
conn.close()
```

Notes

- Make sure to replace placeholders (like your_server_address,
  your_database_name, etc.) with actual values for your database.
- It's good practice to handle exceptions and errors in your database operations,
  using try-except blocks.
- Managing resources using context managers (with statements) is also
  recommended to ensure that connections are properly closed.

4. Connecting to a MySQL Database

Connecting to a MySQL database from Python can be efficiently done using the mysql-connector-python package, which is a MySQL driver written in Python. Here's how you can establish a connection and execute queries on a MySQL database:

Step 1: Install mysql-connector-python

Before you start, ensure that the mysql-connector-python package is installed in your environment. You can install it using pip:

```
pip install mysql-connector-python
```

Step 2: Import mysql.connector

Once installed, you can use it in your Python scripts by importing `mysql.connector`:

```
import mysql.connector
```

Step 3: Create a Connection

To connect to your MySQL database, you'll need to know your database's host address, database name, user name, and password. With this information, you can establish a connection:

```
cnx = mysql.connector.connect(
    host="your_host",
    user="your_username",
    password="your_password",
    database="your_database_name"
)
```

If you are connecting to a database running on the same machine your script is running on, you can use `localhost` for the host.

Step 4: Create a Cursor Object

After establishing a connection, you create a cursor object using the connection. The cursor is used to execute queries.

```
cursor = cnx.cursor()
```

Step 5: Execute SQL Queries

You can now execute SQL queries using the cursor object. For example, to query data:

```
cursor.execute("SELECT * FROM your_table_name")
for row in cursor:
    print(row)
```

To insert data into a table:

```
query = "INSERT INTO your_table_name (column1, column2) VALUES (%s, %s)"
values = ("value1", "value2")
cursor.execute(query, values)
cnx.commit()  # Make sure data is committed to the database
```

Step 6: Close Cursor and Connection

After executing your queries, it's important to close both the cursor and the connection to free up resources:

```
cursor.close()
cnx.close()
```

5. Connecting to an Oracle database

Connecting to an Oracle database from Python typically involves using the `cx_Oracle` library, which is a Python extension module that enables access to Oracle databases. It provides a robust set of features for performing database operations and is widely used in the industry for Oracle database connectivity. Here's how to establish a connection and execute queries:

Step 1: Install cx_Oracle

First, you need to install the `cx_Oracle` module. You can easily install it using pip. Before installing, make sure you have the Oracle Instant Client installed on your system, as `cx_Oracle` depends on it.
Install `cx_Oracle` using pip:

```
pip install cx_Oracle
```

Step 2: Write Python Code to Connect to Oracle

Now, you can write Python code to connect to your Oracle database:

```python
import cx_Oracle

def create_connection():
    # Replace placeholders with your actual Oracle DB credentials
    dsn = cx_Oracle.makedsn('YourDBHost', 'YourDBPort', sid='YourDBSID')
    # Alternatively, use a service name instead of SID:
    # dsn = cx_Oracle.makedsn('YourDBHost', 'YourDBPort',
service_name='YourServiceName')
    connection = cx_Oracle.connect(user='YourUsername',
password='YourPassword', dsn=dsn)

    return connection

def execute_query(connection):
    # Example query
    cursor = connection.cursor()
    cursor.execute("SELECT sysdate FROM dual")
    for row in cursor:
        print("Current date and time in Oracle Database:", row)
    cursor.close()

def main():
    conn = None
    try:
        conn = create_connection()
        execute_query(conn)
    finally:
        if conn is not connected:
            conn.close()

if __name__ == "__main__":
    main()
```

Step 3: Run Your Python Script

Save the above script in a file, say `connect_oracle.py`, and run it from your command line:

```
python connect_oracle.py
```

This script will connect to the Oracle database using the credentials provided, execute a query to retrieve the current date and time from the database, and then close the connection.

Important Considerations

- Ensure that the `cx_Oracle` library and the Oracle Instant Client are compatible with each other.
- Adjust your connection parameters (`dsn, user, password`) to match those of your Oracle Database setup.
- The Oracle Client library path and other configurations must be properly set up for `cx_Oracle` to function correctly.

Chapter 7 Introduction to natural language processing (NLP)

Natural Language Processing (NLP) is a field at the intersection of computer science, artificial intelligence, and linguistics. It focuses on the interaction between computers and humans through natural language. The goal is to enable computers to understand and process human languages in a way that is both valuable and meaningful. NLP involves several steps and techniques to interpret human language, ranging from basic to complex, including tokenization, stemming, and sentiment analysis.

1. What can Natural Language Processing (NLP) be used for

Natural Language Processing (NLP) is a field of artificial intelligence that focuses on the interaction between computers and humans through natural language. Natural language processing (NLP) is critical to fully and efficiently analyze text and speech data. The goal is to read, decipher, understand, and make sense of the human languages in a manner that is valuable. Here are some examples of how NLP is used:

Chatbots and Virtual Assistants:

NLP powers the responses and interactions in virtual assistants like Siri, Alexa, and Google Assistant. These systems use NLP to understand and respond to voice or text commands, providing information or performing actions accordingly.

Sentiment Analysis:

This involves analyzing text from comments, reviews, or social media to determine the sentiment expressed by the speaker or writer. Businesses use this to understand customer opinions and feelings about products or services.

Machine Translation:

Services like Google Translate use NLP to convert text from one language to another. This involves understanding the grammar, style, and vocabulary of both the source and target languages.

Speech Recognition:

NLP is used to convert spoken language into text in real-time in applications like voice-driven text entry or voice control systems.

Content Recommendations:

NLP algorithms analyze your previous activity, preferences, and text descriptions of content to recommend relevant new content, such as books, news articles, or movies.

Information Extraction: NLP can be used to extract specific information from large texts, such as names, places, dates, and other relevant data, helping to structure unstructured data.

Text Summarization:

NLP is used to automatically generate concise summaries of long documents, preserving key information and its overall meaning.

These examples showcase how NLP bridges the gap between human communication and computer understanding, enhancing the convenience and efficiency of many tasks.

2. Applications of NLP in Data Management

NLP can significantly enhance data management systems by enabling more effective information retrieval, organization, and insights extraction:

Information Retrieval:

NLP can improve search functionalities by understanding the context and semantics of queries.

Data Categorization:

Automated categorization of text data based on content, which helps in managing large volumes of unstructured data.

Data Cleaning: NLP can aid in cleaning data by removing irrelevant or redundant information and correcting errors.

Knowledge Extraction:

Extracting useful information and insights from text data, such as trends, patterns, and relationships.

Automated Reporting: Generating summaries or reports from large datasets, which can help in making data-driven decisions faster.

3. Key Techniques in NLP

- **Tokenization:**

  This is the process of breaking down text into smaller pieces, called tokens. Tokens can be words, phrases, or sentences. Tokenization is fundamental in NLP as it helps in simplifying complex text data.

- **Stemming:**

  This involves reducing words to their base or root form. For instance, "running", "runs", and "ran" are all reduced to the root "run". This helps in generalizing different forms of the same word to a single form, aiding in text processing.

- **Sentiment Analysis:**

  This is used to determine the attitude or emotion of the writer, such as positive, negative, or neutral. It's widely used in business for analyzing customer feedback, market research, and social media monitoring.

Implementation with NLTK

The Natural Language Toolkit (NLTK) is a powerful Python library for working with human language data. It provides easy-to-use interfaces to over 50 corpora and lexical resources such as WordNet, along with a suite of text processing libraries for classification, tokenization, stemming, tagging, parsing, and semantic reasoning.

To implement tokenization, stemming, and sentiment analysis using NLTK, we'll need to write some Python code:

- Tokenization: Splitting text into words or sentences. The function tokenize_text takes a string of text and returns both the sentences and words as tokens.
- Stemming: Applying a stemming algorithm. The function stem_words applies stemming to a list of words, reducing each word to its root form using the Porter Stemming Algorithm.
- Sentiment Analysis: Using a pre-trained model within NLTK to determine the sentiment of text. The function analyze_sentiment uses NLTK's Sentiment Intensity Analyzer to evaluate the sentiment of a given text, returning a dictionary with scores for positive, negative, neutral, and compound values (which indicate overall sentiment).

These functions are ready to use on any text input to perform tokenization, stemming, and sentiment analysis respectively. If you have any specific text or further requirements, I can demonstrate these functions with those details.

4. An example of using NLTK

The Natural Language Toolkit (NLTK) is a popular Python library used for working with human language data (text). It provides easy-to-use interfaces to over 50 corpora and lexical resources such as WordNet, along with a suite of text processing libraries for classification, tokenization, stemming, tagging, parsing, and semantic reasoning. Here's an example of how NLTK can be used for a common NLP task: sentiment analysis.

Sentiment Analysis Example with NLTK

In this example, we'll use NLTK to determine the sentiment of a text. We will use the movie reviews corpus available in NLTK, which includes labeled positive and negative reviews. Here's a basic outline of the steps involved:

1. Import Libraries and Data: Load necessary libraries and the movie reviews dataset.
2. Preprocess Data: Tokenize text and create a list of word features.
3. Create Feature Sets: Construct a feature extractor that checks the presence of words in a document.
4. Train a Classifier: Train a Naive Bayes Classifier with these features.
5. Evaluate and Test: Assess the classifier's performance and use it to analyze the sentiment of new texts.

Let's implement this:

This example demonstrates how NLTK can be effectively used for text classification tasks such as sentiment analysis.

```python
import nltk
from nltk.corpus import movie_reviews
from nltk.classify import NaiveBayesClassifier
from nltk.classify.util import accuracy

# Ensure the data is downloaded
nltk.download('movie_reviews')

# Step 1: Prepare the data
documents = [(list(movie_reviews.words(fileid)), category)
            for category in movie_reviews.categories()
            for fileid in movie_reviews.fileids(category)]

# Shuffle the documents for better training and testing
import random
random.shuffle(documents)

# Step 2: Feature Extraction
all_words = nltk.FreqDist(w.lower() for w in movie_reviews.words())
word_features = list(all_words)[:2000]  # Top 2000 words as features

def document_features(document):
    document_words = set(document)
    features = {}
    for word in word_features:
        features[f"contains({word})"] = (word in document_words)
    return features

# Step 3: Create feature sets
feature_sets = [(document_features(d), c) for (d, c) in documents]

# Split into training and test sets
train_set, test_set = feature_sets[100:], feature_sets[:100]

# Step 4: Train a classifier
classifier = NaiveBayesClassifier.train(train_set)

# Step 5: Evaluate the classifier
print(f"Accuracy: {accuracy(classifier, test_set):.2f}")
classifier.show_most_informative_features(5)

# Example usage: Classifying new text
new_text = "This movie is an amazing journey of love and life."
new_features = document_features(new_text.split())
print("Sentiment:", classifier.classify(new_features))
```

In this script, we use the movie reviews dataset to train a Naive Bayes classifier. The feature extractor checks each document to see if it contains one of the most common words found in the overall corpus. Finally, we test the classifier's accuracy on a set of test data and use it to predict the sentiment of a new sentence.

Chapter 8 Automation using Python

Automation using Python is a powerful and versatile approach that allows you to streamline repetitive and time-consuming tasks across a variety of domains such as data analysis, web development, and system administration. Python, with its simple syntax and rich ecosystem of libraries, makes it an ideal language for automation.

Why is Python used for Automation?

- Ease of Learning: Python's syntax is clean and its concepts are easier to grasp compared to other programming languages.
- Extensive Libraries: Python offers a wealth of libraries specifically tailored for automation tasks like **selenium** for web automation, **pandas** for data manipulation, and **pytest** for automating test scripts.
- Community and Support: A large community means more support, shared knowledge, and pre-built tools and modules that you can use to automate tasks.

1. Common Libraries for Automation

- Selenium: Used for automating web browsers, enabling you to perform tasks like testing, web scraping, or automating actions on a web browser.
- Pandas: Excellent for data manipulation and analysis; it can automate the processing of large data sets, perform complex data filtering, transformations, and more.
- Automate: A less known but very useful library that can help automate desktop tasks such as opening files, running programs, or managing file systems.

- Requests: Simplifies making HTTP requests to APIs, useful for automating interactions with web services.

2. Practical Applications of Python Automation

- **Data Aggregation**

  Automating the collection and synthesis of data from various sources into a single, coherent file or database using pandas and requests.

- **Report Generation**

  Scripts can automate the generation of reports by fetching data, analyzing it, and compiling it into PDFs or Excel files using libraries like **ReportLab** or **openpyxl.**

- **Automated Email Responses**

  Using libraries such as **smtplib** and email, Python can automate the sending of email responses to scheduled reports or specific triggers from a web service.

- **Error Handling**

  Always include error handling in your automation scripts to manage unexpected issues gracefully. Use try, except, finally blocks to handle exceptions.

- **Logging:**

Implement logging using Python's logging module to keep track of what your scripts are doing, which is very helpful for debugging and understanding script actions.

- **Security Measures:**

Be cautious with sensitive data. Use environment variables and secure vaults to store credentials, and ensure that your automation scripts are protected from unauthorized access.

3. Examples of using pandas, requests, sqalchemy:

Automating the collection and synthesis of data from various sources into a coherent file or database using Python's pandas library can significantly streamline your workflows. Here's a step-by-step example that demonstrates how you can gather data from different sources like CSV files, APIs, and databases, and then consolidate them into a single pandas DataFrame. For simplicity, we'll assume the data includes user information from different branches of a company

Suppose you need to collect user data from three sources:

1) A CSV file from the HR department: hr_data.csv
2) An API providing user data from the sales team:
3) A SQL database containing user data from the tech department.

make sure you install the following libraries:

```
pip install pandas
pip install requests
pip install sqlalchemy
```

```python
1
2    # step 1 reading user data from a CSV file
3
4    import pandas as pd
5    # Load data from a CSV file
6    hr_data = pd.read_csv('hr_data.csv')
7
8    #Step 2: Fetching Data from an API, use the requests library for making HTTP requests.
9
10   import requests
11
12   def fetch_api_data(url):
13       response = requests.get(url)
14       data = response.json()
15       return pd.DataFrame(data)
16
17   # Assuming the API returns data in JSON format that directly translates to a DataFrame
18   sales_data = fetch_api_data('https://api.company.com/sales/users')
19
20
21   #Step 3: Retrieving Data from a SQL Database by using pandas with SQLAlchemy for database connectivity.
22
23   from sqlalchemy import create_engine
24
25   # Create a connection to the database
26   engine = create_engine('sqlite:///tech_department.db')
27
28   # Execute SQL query and load into DataFrame
29   tech_data = pd.read_sql_query('SELECT * FROM users', engine)
```

```
30
31  #Step 4: Data Synthesis Once all data is loaded into a DataFrames, the next step is to consolidate or merge this da
32  #into a single DataFrame. We will assume that each DataFrame has a common identifier, such as user_id.
33
34  # Merge the DataFrames on 'user_id'
35  all_data = pd.merge(hr_data, sales_data, on='user_id', how='outer')
36  all_data = pd.merge(all_data, tech_data, on='user_id', how='outer')
37
38  # Fill any NaN values with a placeholder or appropriate default
39  all_data.fillna('N/A', inplace=True)
40
41  #Step 5: Analysis or Export
42  # Export to a new CSV file
43  all_data.to_csv('consolidated_user_data.csv', index=False)
44
45  # perform some data analysis
46  print(all_data.describe())
```

4. System time and format

Getting the system time in Python and formatting it according to specific requirements is straightforward with Python's **datetime** module. Here's how you can do it:

You can use the datetime.now()/datetime.today() method from the datetime module to get the current date and time.The strftime() method is used to format datetime objects into readable strings. It takes a format string that specifies how the datetime should be formatted.

Example 1 To get different date format

Example2: Here's a simple script that demonstrates how to get the current system time and format it in a couple of different ways:

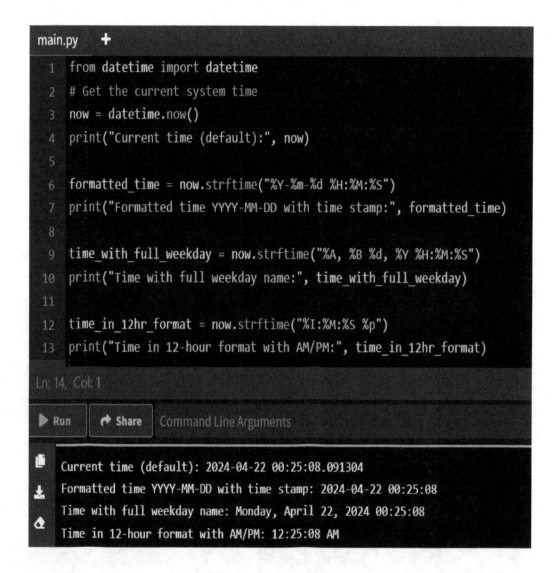

```python
from datetime import datetime
# Get the current system time
now = datetime.now()
print("Current time (default):", now)

formatted_time = now.strftime("%Y-%m-%d %H:%M:%S")
print("Formatted time YYYY-MM-DD with time stamp:", formatted_time)

time_with_full_weekday = now.strftime("%A, %B %d, %Y %H:%M:%S")
print("Time with full weekday name:", time_with_full_weekday)

time_in_12hr_format = now.strftime("%I:%M:%S %p")
print("Time in 12-hour format with AM/PM:", time_in_12hr_format)
```

```
Current time (default): 2024-04-22 00:25:08.091304
Formatted time YYYY-MM-DD with time stamp: 2024-04-22 00:25:08
Time with full weekday name: Monday, April 22, 2024 00:25:08
Time in 12-hour format with AM/PM: 12:25:08 AM
```

Explanation of strftime() Format Codes:

- %Y: Year with century as a decimal number.
- %m: Month as a decimal number [01,12].
- %d: Day of the month as a decimal number [01,31].
- %H: Hour (24-hour clock) as a decimal number [00,23].

- %M: Minute as a decimal number [00,59].

- %S: Second as a decimal number [00,61].

- %A: Locale's full weekday name.

- %B: Locale's full month name.

- %I: Hour (12-hour clock) as a decimal number [01,12].

- %p: Locale's equivalent of either AM or PM.

These formatting options make it easy to customize the datetime representation to fit the needs of different applications, whether it's for logging, displaying to users, or any other purpose.

Example 3 covers the following cases:

- **Time Zone Handling:**

Python's datetime module can handle time zones with the help of the pytz library or the zoneinfo module (available from Python 3.9). Managing time zones is crucial for applications that operate across different geographic locations.

- **Date Arithmetic:**

Perform operations like adding or subtracting days, weeks, or months from a date. This is useful for generating dates for schedules, forecasts, or reminders.

- **Difference Between Dates:**

Calculate the time difference between two dates to find durations or measure time intervals.

- **Handling Date and Time Formats from User Input:**

Convert string representations of dates and times into datetime objects, and vice versa, to interface with user input or databases.

Script for Example 3

```
1    from datetime import datetime, timedelta
2    from dateutil.relativedelta import relativedelta
3    import pytz
4    from zoneinfo import ZoneInfo  # For Python 3.9 and above
5
6    # Time Zone Handling
7    utc_now = datetime.now(pytz.utc)  # UTC time
8    local_now = utc_now.astimezone(pytz.timezone('America/New_York'))  # Convert to Eastern Time
9
10   # Date Arithmetic
11   tomorrow = datetime.now() + timedelta(days=1)  # Tomorrow's date
12   next_month = datetime.now() + relativedelta(months=1)  # Next month's date
13
14   # Difference Between Dates
15   date1 = datetime(2023, 1, 1)
16   date2 = datetime(2024, 1, 1)
17
18   difference = date2 - date1  # Difference between dates
19   days_difference = difference.days  # Difference in days
20
21   # Formatting for Display
22   formatted_date = local_now.strftime("%Y-%m-%d %H:%M:%S %Z")
23   print("Current time in Eastern Time with zone:", formatted_date)
24   # Handling Date and Time Formats from User Input
25   date_input = "2023-04-01"
26   date_object = datetime.strptime(date_input, "%Y-%m-%d")  # Convert string to datetime
27   formatted_back = date_object.strftime("%B %d, %Y")  # Convert datetime back to string
28   print("Formatted date from input:", formatted_back)
29   # Displaying advanced calculations
30   print("Tomorrow's date:", tomorrow)
31   print("Next month's date:", next_month)
32   print("Days difference between two dates:", days_difference)
```

Explanation for libraries used in example3:

- pytz: Manages time zone conversions.
- dateutil.relativedelta: Allows more complex date manipulations like adding months or years, which aren't supported by timedelta.

5. Handling leap year

Handling leap years efficiently in Python can be crucial for a variety of applications, such as scheduling, forecasting, and ensuring date calculations are accurate. Here's how you can determine if a year is a leap year and work with leap year data:

Criteria for a Leap Year:

A year is a leap year if:

1. It is divisible by 4.
2. It is not divisible by 100 unless it is also divisible by 400.

This means that years like 2000 and 2400 are leap years, but 1800 and 1900 are not.

Python Methods to Handle Leap Years:

Python's calendar module provides a function called isleap() that returns True if the year is a leap year, and False otherwise. This simplifies the process, so you don't have to manually implement the rules.

Example Script to Work with Leap Years:

Here's a script that demonstrates how to determine if a specific year is a leap year, and how to perform operations related to leap years.

```python
import calendar

def is_leap_year(year):
    """Return True if the year is a leap year, False otherwise."""
    return calendar.isleap(year)

def days_in_year(year):
    """Return the number of days in a given year."""
    return 366 if is_leap_year(year) else 365

def next_leap_year(start_year):
    """Find the next leap year after the given start year."""
    year = start_year
    while not is_leap_year(year):
        year += 1
    return year

# Example usage:
year_to_check = 2024
print(f"Is {year_to_check} a leap year? {is_leap_year(year_to_check)}")
print(f"Days in {year_to_check}: {days_in_year(year_to_check)}")
print(f"Next leap year after {year_to_check}: {next_leap_year(year_to_check + 1)}")
```

Script Explanation:

- is_leap_year(year): Utilizes the calendar.isleap() method to determine if a year is a leap year.

- days_in_year(year): Returns 366 if the year is a leap year, otherwise returns 365.

- next_leap_year(start_year): Continues to increment the year until it finds a leap year, starting from the provided start_year.

6. Automate Repetitive Tasks

Python can be used to automate a wide variety of repetitive tasks. Let's see an example of file management task:

6.1 File Management task: Automating the process of monthly copying, moving, renaming files with time stamp from source folder to destination folder, also need a report for logging or reporting the results of these operations.

Designing process:

1. Copying Files: Copy files from one folder to another with a timestamp.
   *Identify Source and Destination: Define the source and destination directories.
   *Key-Value Path System: The source and destination paths can now be dynamically selected based on a dictionary key. This makes it easy to manage different sets of folders by just changing the key.

2. Moving Files: Move files after copying to ensure they're not processed again in the next run.
   *Identify Source and Destination: Define the source and destination directories.

3. Timestamping: Use the current date and time to timestamp files with the timestamp appended to filenames now includes only the date in the yyyymmdd format.

4. Renaming Files: Append a timestamp to the filenames to maintain uniqueness and traceability.

5. Logging: Generate a report that logs the details of the operations, including successes and any errors encountered.

Here is the python script for our task. Please make sure to install all the libraries used and replace the file path and folder name with your path and folder name.

```
1
2    import os
3    import shutil
4    from datetime import datetime
5    import logging
6
7    # Define paths using a dictionary to dynamically determine them based on a key
8    folders = {
9        'test': ('/path/to/your/source/folder', '/path/to/your/destination/folder'),
10   }
11
12   # Setup logging
13   logging.basicConfig(filename='file_operations_log.txt', level=logging.INFO,
14                       format='%(asctime)s:%(levelname)s:%(message)s')
15
16   def timestamp_filename(filename):
17       """Append the current date to the filename."""
18       base, extension = os.path.splitext(filename)
19       current_date = datetime.now().strftime("%Y%m%d")
20       new_filename = f"{base}_{current_date}{extension}"
21       return new_filename
```

```python
22
23   def copy_and_rename_files(source, destination):
24       """Copy files from the source directory to the destination directory with a datestamp."""
25       files = os.listdir(source)
26       for file in files:
27           full_file_path = os.path.join(source, file)
28           if os.path.isfile(full_file_path):
29               new_filename = timestamp_filename(file)
30               dest_file_path = os.path.join(destination, new_filename)
31               try:
32                   shutil.copy(full_file_path, dest_file_path)
33                   logging.info(f"Successfully copied {file} to {new_filename}")
34               except Exception as e:
35                   logging.error(f"Failed to copy {file}. Error: {e}")
36
37   def move_files(source, destination):
38       """Move files from the source directory to the destination to prevent re-processing."""
39       files = os.listdir(source)
40       for file in files:
41           full_file_path = os.path.join(source, file)
42           if os.path.isfile(full_file_path):
43               new_filename = timestamp_filename(file)
44               dest_file_path = os.path.join(destination, new_filename)
45               try:
46                   shutil.move(full_file_path, dest_file_path)
47                   logging.info(f"Successfully moved {file} to {new_filename}")
48               except Exception as e:
49                   logging.error(f"Failed to move {file}. Error: {e}")
50
51   # Example of how to use the function with keys:
52   key = 'test'
53   copy_and_rename_files(*folders[key])
54   move_files(*folders[key])
```

Example 4: File management for multiple level directory. We will rename files based on key values in source folder, then add date in the new file name, copy files to destination

```python
import os
import shutil
import pandas as pd
import random
#global random number for transaction_id
#transaction_id = random.randint(60000,65000)
transaction_id = 60000
#global_df = pd.DataFrame()
print(transaction_id)
from datetime import datetime
#df['new_column']= datetime.today().strftime('%Y-%m-%d')
subdate= datetime.today().strftime('%Y%m%d')
#print(subdate)
#####################################################
# Step 1: Copy all files to destination
#####################################################
def search_copy_rename_save(source_dir, destination_dir, key_value,
FileCategory):
        file_info_list = []  # List to store information about copied and renamed files
        #transaction_id = 60000  # Initial transaction ID
        global transaction_id
  # date = date()
        for root, dirs, files in os.walk(source_dir):
        for folder in dirs:
        if key_value in folder:
                folder_path = os.path.join(root, folder)
                for file in os.listdir(folder_path):
                file_path = os.path.join(folder_path, file)
                # if any(keyword in file for keyword in
['txt','FILE.RPT','ZZZZ','XYXY']):  # Check if file name contains any of the
keywords
                if any(keyword in file for keyword in ['txt']):  # Check if file name
contains any of the keywords
                #partial_info = extract_partial_info(file)
                parts = file.split('_')

                sourceFileType = parts[1][-4:]
                new_file_name =  "YYYY_" + parts[1][-4:] + "_AAAA_" +
f"{subdate}" + "_" + f"{transaction_id}" + ".dat"
                new_file_path = os.path.join(destination_dir, new_file_name)
                FileType = "AAAA"+parts[1][-4:]
                shutil.copy(file_path, new_file_path)
                print(f"Copied '{file}' to '{new_file_path}'")

                # Store file information into a dictionary
                file_info = {
                        "source_folder": folder_path,
                        "sourceFileType": sourceFileType,
                        "source_path": file_path,
```

```python
                            "old_file_name": file,
                            "destination_path": new_file_path,
                            "new_file_name": new_file_name,
                            "FileType": FileType ,
                            "sourceFileType": sourceFileType
                    }
                    file_info_list.append(file_info)

                    # Increment transaction ID for the next file
                    transaction_id += 1
                elif any(keyword in file for keyword in ['DATPRS_FILE.RPT']):
                    #partial_info = extract_partial_info(file)
                    parts = file.split('.')
                    #pdt=parts[3].split(".")

                    sourceFileType ="M2"
                    new_file_name =  "YYYY_DATPRS_AAAA_" +  f"{subdate}" +"_" +
f"{transaction_id}" + ".dat"
                    new_file_path = os.path.join(destination_dir, new_file_name)
                    FileType = "AAAADATPRS"
                    shutil.copy(file_path, new_file_path)
                    # print(f"Copied '{file}' to '{new_file_path}'")

                    # Store file information into a dictionary
                    file_info = {
                            "source_folder": folder_path,
                            "sourceFileType": sourceFileType,
                            "source_path": file_path,
                            "old_file_name": file,
                            "destination_path": new_file_path,
                            "new_file_name": new_file_name,
                            "FileType": FileType
                    }
                    file_info_list.append(file_info)

                    # Increment transaction ID for the next file
                    transaction_id += 1
                elif any(keyword in file for keyword in ['DATDUP_FILE.RPT']):
                    #partial_info = extract_partial_info(file)
                    parts = file.split('.')
                    #pdt=parts[3].split(".")

                    sourceFileType = "M1"
                    new_file_name = "YYYY_DATDUP_AAAA_" + f"{subdate}" +"_" +
f"{transaction_id}" + ".dat"
                    new_file_path = os.path.join(destination_dir, new_file_name)
                    FileType = "AAAADATDUP"
                    shutil.copy(file_path, new_file_path)
                    print(f"Copied '{file}' to '{new_file_path}'")
```

```python
        # Store file information into a dictionary
        file_info = {
                "source_folder": folder_path,
                "sourceFileType": sourceFileType,
                "source_path": file_path,
                "old_file_name": file,
                "destination_path": new_file_path,
                "new_file_name": new_file_name,
                "FileType": FileType
        }
        file_info_list.append(file_info)

        # Increment transaction ID for the next file
        transaction_id += 1
        elif any(keyword in file for keyword in ['ZZZZCA']):
        #partial_info = extract_partial_info(file)
        parts = file.split('.')
          #pdt=parts[3].split(".")

          sourceFileType ="ZZZZCA"
        new_file_name =  "YYYY_ZZZZ_AAAA_" +  f"{subdate}"  +"_" +
f"{transaction_id}" + ".dat"
        new_file_path = os.path.join(destination_dir, new_file_name)
        FileType = "AAAAZZZZ"

        shutil.copy(file_path, new_file_path)
        print(f"Copied '{file}' to '{new_file_path}'")

        # Store file information into a dictionary
        file_info = {
                "source_folder":folder_path,
                "sourceFileType":sourceFileType,
                "source_path": file_path,
                "old_file_name": file,
                "destination_path": new_file_path,
                "new_file_name": new_file_name,
                "FileType":FileType
            #"Upload Date": date
        }
        file_info_list.append(file_info)

        # Increment transaction ID for the next file
        transaction_id += 1
        elif  any(keyword in file for keyword in ['XYXY']):
                #partial_info = extract_partial_info(file)
                parts = file.split('.')
            # pdt=parts[3].split(".")
```

```python
                        sourceFileType = "XYXY"
                        new_file_name =  "YYYY_" + "XYXY_AAAA_" +
f"{subdate}"  +"_" + f"{transaction_id}" + ".dat"
                        new_file_path = os.path.join(destination_dir,
new_file_name)

                        FileType = "AAAAXYXY"

                    shutil.copy(file_path, new_file_path)
                        print(f"Copied '{file}' to '{new_file_path}'")

                    # Store file information into a dictionary
                        file_info = {
                        "source_folder": folder_path,
                        "sourceFileType": sourceFileType,
                        "source_path": file_path,
                        "old_file_name": file,
                        "destination_path": new_file_path,
                        "new_file_name": new_file_name,
                        "FileType":  FileType
                        }
                        file_info_list.append(file_info)

                    # Increment transaction ID for the next file
                        transaction_id += 1
                elif  any(keyword in file for keyword in ['REJECT']):
                        #partial_info = extract_partial_info(file)
                        parts = file.split('.')
                    # pdt=parts[3].split(".")

                    sourceFileType = "REJECT"
                        new_file_name =  "YYYY_REJECT_AAAA_" +  f"{subdate}"
+"_" + f"{transaction_id}" + ".dat"
                        new_file_path = os.path.join(destination_dir,
new_file_name)

                        FileType = "AAAAREJECT"

                    shutil.copy(file_path, new_file_path)
                        print(f"Copied '{file}' to '{new_file_path}'")

                    # Store file information into a dictionary
                        file_info = {
                        "source_folder": folder_path,
                        "sourceFileType": sourceFileType,
                        "source_path": file_path,
                        "old_file_name": file,
                        "destination_path": new_file_path,
                        "new_file_name": new_file_name,
                        "FileType":  FileType
                        }
```

```python
        file_info_list.append(file_info)

    # Increment transaction ID for the next file
    transaction_id += 1
# Convert file_info list into a pandas DataFrame
df = pd.DataFrame(file_info_list)

# Save DataFrame to a CSV file
df.to_csv("folder2//file_info.csv", index=False)
print("File information saved to 'file_info.csv'")




######################################################################
        Step2 :Get the final file list by only keeping last XYXY file per folder

######################################################################
    #check XYXY multiple files in each folder if so, only keep the last one
    df_XYXY = df[df["new_file_name"].str.contains("XYXY")]
    print("XYXY",df_XYXY)
# Sort the DataFrame by 'Value' column in descending order if nesccesary
    #df_sorted = df.sort_values(by='Value', ascending=False)

    # Keep the last record per group
    df_XYXY_Last = df_XYXY.groupby('source_folder').tail(1)
    print("XYXY",df_XYXY_Last)


    print("test last_filename",df_XYXY_Last)

mask =df["new_file_name"].str.contains("XYXY", case=False)
    # Invert the mask to get rows not containing the keyword
    inverted_mask = ~mask
    # Subset  DataFrame using the inverted mask
    df_other = df[inverted_mask]

    #print("other",df_other)

df_to_send =  pd.concat([df_other,  df_XYXY_Last  ], ignore_index=True)
    #df_to_send['new_column']= datetime.today().strftime('%Y-%m-%d')
    df_to_send['FileCategory']= FileCategory
    #df_other.to_csv("folder1.csv", index=False)
    df_to_send.to_csv("folder2/Final_filelist_info.csv", index=False)


# Example usage:
#AAAA\AAAA\Prod\Institutional\2023_Mar_01_dn
source_directory = "source folder//AAAA/Prod/Institutional/"
#source_directory = "source_folder/AAAA"
```

```
destination_directory = "destination folder name"
#key_value = "202"
#key_value = "2023"
#key_value = "2023_Mar_01_dn"
FileCategory ="Institutional"
search_copy_rename_save(source_directory, destination_directory,
key_value,FileCategory)
```

6.2 Data Processing task:

Automatically cleaning, processing, and analyzing multiple datasets.

Here is a real task of gathering data from multiple csv and json files .

To automate the process of gathering data from multiple CSV and JSON files,
combining them, and comparing data from the previous month.

Coding plan:

Requirements Overview:

1. Data Collection: Automate the reading of multiple CSV and JSON files.
2. Data Combination: Combine these datasets into a single data structure.
3. Data Comparison: Dynamically compare specific columns with data from the
   previous month.
4. Reporting or Output: Possibly generate a summary report or output detailing
   the comparisons.

Python Libraries and Tools:

- Pandas: Ideal for handling data manipulation tasks like reading files, merging
  datasets, and comparing data columns.
- Numpy: Useful for numerical operations that might be required during data
  comparison.

- Glob: To find all the file paths matching a specified pattern, making it easier to handle multiple files.

Step-by-Step Breakdown:

1. Identify File Locations: Establish paths where the CSV and JSON files are stored.
2. Read Files: Use Pandas to read files monthly as they become available.
3. Merge Data: Combine data from these files into a single DataFrame. This step may involve standardizing column names and data formats.
4. Compare Data: Implement logic to compare the data in the specified columns with the previous month's data.
5. Generate Output: Summarize the results of the comparison in an output format suitable for your needs, such as a CSV file, a report, or simply logging the findings.

Example Workflow:

- Each month, the script runs (possibly scheduled with a cron job or Windows Task Scheduler).
- It loads all CSV and JSON files from specified directories.
- Processes and merges these files based on predefined logic.
- Compares the relevant columns with the data from the previous month (this implies storing or accessing previous month's data).
- Outputs the comparison results.

Basic script outline that handles the initial steps of your data processing automation task:

1. Reading CSV Files: The function read_csv_files reads all CSV files matching a given pattern and combines them into a single DataFrame.
2. Reading JSON Files: The function read_json_files reads all JSON files, loads their contents, and combines them into another DataFrame.

3. Combining Data: The combine_data function merges the data from both CSV and JSON sources into one DataFrame.

Key Functions:

- glob.glob(path_pattern): Finds all file paths in a directory that match a certain pattern, useful for loading multiple files.
- pd.read_csv(file): Reads a CSV file into a Pandas DataFrame.
- pd.concat(df_list, ignore_index=True): Merges multiple DataFrames into one.

Next Steps:

The next steps in the development process will involve:

- Standardizing and cleaning the data to ensure consistency across columns from different files.
- Implementing logic to compare data dynamically with previous months. This will likely require some way to reference or store past data.
- Outputting the results of the comparison, either in a report format or as summarized data.
- Load Previous Month Data:
  - Loads data from a specified file, intended to be the previous month's data, allowing for dynamic comparisons.
- Compare Data:
  - Compares specific columns between the current and previous month's data to identify changes. This uses a merge operation to find differences and can be customized based on the columns you wish to compare.
- Save Data:
  - Saves the current month's data and any changes found during comparison into CSV files for future reference or reporting.

Detailed Explanation:

- Merging and Comparison: The comparison function merges the current and previous datasets on specified columns and flags rows that do not match perfectly, indicating changes or new entries.
- Data Storage and Retrieval: By saving the current month's data, you establish a historical record that can be loaded in subsequent runs to compare against new data.

```python
import pandas as pd
import glob
import json
import os

def read_csv_files(path_pattern):
    """Read multiple CSV files and combine them into a single DataFrame."""
    csv_files = glob.glob(path_pattern)
    df_list = [pd.read_csv(file) for file in csv_files]
    combined_df = pd.concat(df_list, ignore_index=True)
    return combined_df

def read_json_files(path_pattern):
    """Read multiple JSON files and combine them into a single DataFrame."""
    json_files = glob.glob(path_pattern)
    df_list = []
    for file in json_files:
        with open(file, 'r') as f:
            data = json.load(f)
            df_list.append(pd.DataFrame(data))
    combined_df = pd.concat(df_list, ignore_index=True)
    return combined_df

def combine_data(csv_path_pattern, json_path_pattern):
    """Combine data from CSV and JSON files into a single DataFrame."""
    csv_df = read_csv_files(csv_path_pattern)
    json_df = read_json_files(json_path_pattern)
    combined_df = pd.concat([csv_df, json_df], ignore_index=True)
    return combined_df
```

```python
def load_previous_month_data(file_path):
    """Load the DataFrame from a CSV file for the previous month's data."""
    if os.path.exists(file_path):
        return pd.read_csv(file_path)
    else:
        return pd.DataFrame()


def compare_data(current_data, previous_data, columns):
    """Compare specified columns between current and previous month's data."""
    if not previous_data.empty:
        comparison_df = pd.merge(current_data, previous_data, on=columns, how='outer', indicator=True)
        changes = comparison_df[comparison_df['_merge'] != 'both']
        return changes
    else:
        return pd.DataFrame()


def save_data(data, file_path):
    """Save the DataFrame to a CSV file."""
    data.to_csv(file_path, index=False)


# Example usage (commented for safety):
current_month_data = combine_data('/path/to/csv/files/*.csv', '/path/to/json/files/*.json')
previous_month_data = load_previous_month_data('/path/to/previous/data.csv')
changes = compare_data(current_month_data, previous_month_data, ['column1', 'column2'])
save_data(current_month_data, '/path/to/save/current/data.csv') # Saving current data for future comparison
save_data(changes, '/path/to/save/changes.csv') # Saving changes report
```

Usage:

- This script should be scheduled to run monthly, processing new CSV and JSON files as they are placed in designated directories.
- It's crucial to update the paths in the example usage comments to point to your actual data locations.
- To fully deploy this, you will need to specify the paths to your data files and decide on the columns to compare.

7. Scheduled Tasks: Running scripts at scheduled times.

Consider setting up a scheduled task (using cron jobs on Linux/macOS or Task Scheduler on Windows) to automate the monthly execution of this script.

Here's how you can do it for both Windows and Linux:

For Windows:

You can use the Windows Task Scheduler to run the Python script monthly:

1. Search for "Task Scheduler" in the Start menu and open it.
2. Create a New Task:
- Go to Action > Create Task in the Task Scheduler.
- Name the task and provide a description.
- Under the Security options, choose the appropriate user account under which the task should run.
- Set it to *Run* whether the user is logged on or not for automation without needing to be logged in.
3. Set the Trigger:
- Go to the Triggers tab and click New.
- Set the task to start On a schedule.

- Choose Monthly and specify the day and time that suits your needs (e.g., every first day of the month at 2 AM).

4. Set the Action:

- Go to the Actions tab and click New.
- Choose Start a program.
- In the Program/script box, type the path to your Python executable (e.g., C:\Python39\python.exe).
- In Add arguments (optional), type the path to your script (e.g., C:\path\to\your\script.py).
- In Start in (optional), enter the directory that contains your script.

5. Finish and Test:

- Go to the Conditions and Settings tabs to further customize the task behavior according to your needs.
- Save the task and right-click it in the Task Scheduler library to choose Run for an initial test.

For Linux:

On a Linux system, you can use cron to schedule the script:

1. Open Terminal.
2. Edit the crontab:

   Type crontab -e to edit the crontab for the current user.

3. Add a cron job:

   Add a line to the crontab file to specify when and how often the script should run.

   /usr/bin/python3 /path/to/your/script.py

   Make sure to replace /usr/bin/python3 with the path to your Python executable, and /path/to/your/script.py with the path to your script.

4. Save and exit: Save the crontab file and exit the editor. Cron will automatically begin to use the new schedule.

Final Setup:

Make sure your script is executable and tested, and that you have all the necessary Python libraries installed. Also, confirm that the Python and script paths are correct in the scheduler settings.

8. Sending automated emails or notifications.

Step-by-Step Guide to Sending Emails.

Step1. Set Up Your Email Credentials:

You'll need access to an SMTP server. This could be your organization's SMTP server or a public email service like Gmail, Outlook, etc. If you're using a public email service, make sure to enable settings that allow you to use their SMTP for sending emails from scripts (e.g., "Less secure app access" in Gmail, which is generally discouraged unless necessary).

Step2. Compose the Email:

The email is composed of a subject, a body, and can optionally include attachments. For simplicity, this example will cover sending a plain text email.

Step3. Send the Email:

Connect to the SMTP server, authenticate, and send the email. Handle exceptions to manage errors effectively.

Example Python Script:

Below is a Python script to send a simple plain text email. Replace placeholders with your actual SMTP settings and credentials.

```python
import smtplib
from email.mime.text import MIMEText
from email.mime.multipart import MIMEMultipart

def send_email(subject, body, to_emails):
    smtp_server = "smtp.example.com"  # Your SMTP server
    smtp_port = 587  # SMTP port (commonly 587 for TLS)
    smtp_user = "your-email@example.com"  # Your email address
    smtp_password = "yourpassword"  # Your email password

    msg = MIMEMultipart()
    msg['From'] = smtp_user
    msg['To'] = ', '.join(to_emails)
    msg['Subject'] = subject

    msg.attach(MIMEText(body, 'plain'))

    try:
        server = smtplib.SMTP(smtp_server, smtp_port)
        server.starttls()  # Start TLS encryption
        server.login(smtp_user, smtp_password)
        text = msg.as_string()
        server.sendmail(smtp_user, to_emails, text)
        server.quit()
        return "Email sent successfully!"
    except Exception as e:
        return f"Failed to send email: {e}"

# Example usage
response = send_email("Hello from Python", "This is a test email sent by Python script.", ["recipient@example.com"])
print(response)
```

Testing and Deployment:

- Testing: Before deploying, test the script with your own email to ensure it works correctly.
- Deployment: You can deploy this script on your server or schedule it to run at specific intervals using cron jobs or task schedulers, depending on your operating system.

Security Considerations:

- If you're using Gmail or another service that requires enabling less secure apps to access SMTP, consider creating a specific email account for this purpose, or better yet, use OAuth2.0 if possible.
- Never hard-code your credentials in your scripts. Instead, use environment variables or encrypted secrets management services.

Steps to Use Gmail SMTP with App-Specific Passwords:

1. Enable Two-Factor Authentication (2FA): Set up 2FA on your Google account.
2. Generate an App-Specific Password:
- Go to your Google Account settings.
- In the "Security" section, look for "Signing in to Google."
- Select "App passwords."
- Follow the prompts to generate a new app password specifically for use with your email script.

Email Script Adjustments for Gmail:

Update the SMTP server details to match Gmail's settings and use the app-specific password generated above.

```python
import smtplib
from email.mime.text import MIMEText
from email.mime.multipart import MIMEMultipart


def send_gmail(subject, body, to_emails):
    smtp_server = "smtp.gmail.com"  # Gmail SMTP server
    smtp_port = 587  # Gmail SMTP port using TLS
    smtp_user = "your-email@gmail.com"  # Your Gmail address
    smtp_password = "app-specific-password"  # Your app-specific password


    msg = MIMEMultipart()
    msg['From'] = smtp_user
    msg['To'] = ', '.join(to_emails)
    msg['Subject'] = subject


    msg.attach(MIMEText(body, 'plain'))

    try:
        server = smtplib.SMTP(smtp_server, smtp_port)
        server.starttls()  # Start TLS encryption
        server.login(smtp_user, smtp_password)
        text = msg.as_string()
        server.sendmail(smtp_user, to_emails, text)
        server.quit()
        return "Email sent successfully!"
    except Exception as e:
        return f"Failed to send email: {e}"


# Example usage
response = send_gmail("Hello from Python", "This is a test email sent by Python script.", ["recipient@example.com"])
print(response)
```

Best Practices and Security:

- Security: Using app-specific passwords is safer than using your main Gmail password but less secure than using OAuth 2.0. If you're planning to integrate this into a production environment or require a higher level of security, consider implementing OAuth 2.0.
- Rate Limits: Be aware of Gmail's rate limits to avoid your account being flagged for unusual activity.

Testing and Deployment:

- Test this script in a controlled environment first to ensure everything works as expected.
- When deploying, ensure your script's environment is secure, especially where your credentials are stored.

Reference:

https://www.python.org/

https://pandas.pydata.org/docs/

https://numpy.org/doc/

https://www.nltk.org/

https://docs.sqlalchemy.org/

https://requests.readthedocs.io/en/lates

https://beautiful-soup-4.readthedocs.io/en/latest/